SOARING

SOARING

ELEVEN GUIDING PRINCIPLES ON THE PATH FROM SEGREGATION TO SUCCESS

BY **LEE E. RHYANT**
AND **CATHERINE M. LEWIS**

FOREWORD BY **SENATOR JOHNNY ISAKSON**

THE UNIVERSITY OF GEORGIA PRESS ATHENS

Library of Congress Cataloging-in-Publication Data

Names: Rhyant, Lee E., author. | Lewis, Catherine M., author.
Title: Soaring : eleven guiding principles on the path from segregation to
    success / by Lee E. Rhyant and Catherine M. Lewis ; foreword by Senator
    Johnny Isakson.
Description: Athens : The University of Georgia Press, [2022] |
    Includes bibliographical references.
Identifiers: LCCN 2021033416 | ISBN 9780820361543 (hardback) |
    ISBN 9780820361550 (ebook)
Subjects: LCSH: Rhyant, Lee E. | African American executives—Biography. |
    African American businesspeople—Biography. | Racism—United States. |
    Success in business—United States.
Classification: LCC HC102.5.R488 A3 2022 | DDC 338.092 [B]—dc22
LC record available at https://lccn.loc.gov/2021033416

CONTENTS

FOREWORD

JOHNNY ISAKSON

I HAVE KNOWN Lee Rhyant for nearly twenty years, and our lives have overlapped in some interesting ways. I am proud to call him a friend and colleague and am thrilled that he is finally writing his memoir. Lee likes to fly under the radar, and most people do not realize how influential and effective he is. This book will change that.

I was born in Atlanta during World War II, and my father was a Greyhound bus driver who later went into real estate. After graduating from the University of Georgia in 1966, I opened the first Cobb County office for Northside Realty and became president in 1979. But it was my work with the Cobb County Chamber of Commerce and as a member of Congress that introduced me to Lee.

I was in the U.S. House of Representatives from 1999 to 2005, and Lee lived and worked in my district. He served as executive vice president and general manager for the Marietta, Georgia, facility of Lockheed Martin Aeronautics Company from July 2000 through January 2011. Lockheed was one of the state's major employers, and so the county and the state always paid a lot of attention to the leadership team. We could not have been luckier to have had Lee at the helm. He offered steady, collaborative, principled leadership that helped the company and the state of Georgia weather some pretty difficult times. During those years, he and I had candid discussions about the possibility of the plant closing and the importance of securing Pentagon contracts for the c-130Js and the f-22 fighter planes. He skillfully led this billion-dollar operation through crisis, change, and prosperity.

One story I recall about Lee always makes me smile. My company, Northside Realty, sold a house to Lee and his wife, Evelyn, in 2000 when he came to work at Lockheed. They had been having a problem with the builder, and one day, my assistant patched a call through from Evelyn. She explained that she had been trying to get a crack in the sidewalk fixed and the builder wasn't being responsive. I was happy to help but explained that this was a recurring problem in the South because of the heat and humidity. We could fix it, but it would likely happen again. That night, she explained to Lee that she had called me. The next thing I know, Lee's on the phone apologizing for the request, knowing that I was busy. I stopped him and said, "Look, you and Evelyn are our customers. I want to treat you right, and I'm never too busy to fix something."

To know Lee is to like him. He is affable, profoundly smart, and so much fun to be around. I share two great loves with him—football and family. When our schedules allow, we talk football and have taken several road trips. In 2012, not long after he retired from Lockheed, I took him to a Georgia football game in Athens. Now, Lee grew up in Florida, and though he had been living in Atlanta for over a decade, he was not yet a Bulldog fan. We sat in the president's suite, lunched on pimento cheese sandwiches, and found that we had a lot of common ground. It helped that the Bulldogs won 51–44, in a thrilling game in which Georgia never relinquished the lead. I am convinced that I converted him to Bulldog Nation that day, and our families have remained close ever since.

This book will resonate with readers who are motivated by underdog stories. Lee was born at the height of the Jim Crow era, overcame prejudice and obstacles that most of us could hardly imagine, pursued undergraduate and graduate degrees against the odds, and did the hard work in business to become one of the leaders of one of the nation's most prestigious companies. I am proud to write the foreword to this book and to introduce Lee to those of you who do not yet know him. I think you will be as inspired by his story as I have been.

Johnny Isakson is a successful businessman with more than forty years of experience in the real estate industry. He served in the U.S. House of Representatives for the Sixth District in Georgia from 1999 to 2004, and his service to the U.S. Senate lasted from 2005 to 2019.

PROLOGUE
KATHY SCHWAIG

I WAS FIRST INTRODUCED to Lee Rhyant when serving as dean of the Coles College of Business at Kennesaw State University. Our college has always had strong connections to political, corporate, and nonprofit leaders, and I was excited to learn more about Lee's work. He had just recently retired from Lockheed Martin in Marietta, and our first conversation focused on how he planned to stay an active and engaged member of the metro Atlanta business and philanthropic community. Sensing an opportunity, I invited him to join the Coles College Advisory Board, and it is one of the best decisions I have ever made. This was a committed group of highly successful men and women, and he became one of the most engaged and strategic members. Lee demonstrated an uncanny ability to help us think critically about how our academic programs connected to workplace trends. He helped craft several important initiatives and I found his counsel invaluable. I always felt that Lee saw a good leader in me but knew I could be better. He decided to mentor me without my even asking. I did not even realize what he was doing until after we had had a few marathon breakfast meetings.

I loved our occasional mornings together and always knew to block off my calendar for at least two or three hours. We would sit down, and he would start talking about what seemed like a series of random topics. Lee is a compelling storyteller, and so I would just sit back and enjoy the ride. I sometimes came prepared with a loose set of questions or issues that I wanted to share, but I rarely had a formal agenda. We would talk, drink coffee, and laugh, and at some point in the conversation, I would pull a notebook out of my purse to take notes. He always loved that, and I came to see that there was a clear method to his approach. What seemed like a series of circuitous, casual anecdotes and observations was always seeded with profound insight and wisdom that he wanted to impart. Taking notes helped me start to see the scaffold of the conversations. I am a pretty linear thinker, and Lee was trying to get me to challenge my assumptions and consider unconventional solutions.

I started to think about our breakfasts as a kind of Lee Rhyant Development Class. Lee has a warm and folksy persona that makes you feel like you are hanging out with your favorite cousin or uncle, but underneath is a keenly strategic mind that is driven by a clear purpose. One morning, Lee inadvertently sent me an email outlining his agenda for breakfast. I had no idea that he had each conversation planned out in his head and was very intentional about addressing issues that he thought were important to me. He had a goal for every session, but he delivered it in such a relational way that it was almost invisible. I realized early on that nothing is random with Lee. You may not know where the journey is going to take you, but you might as well just pack your bags because you are going to be on his train. He is masterful, and his ability to blend leadership lessons and mentoring with skillful storytelling is part of what makes his story and this book so compelling.

Lee's boundless generosity and strategic mind make him indispensable for any institution he serves, and that became the case for Kennesaw State. His service on the Coles College advisory board was just the beginning. He joined KSU's Athletic Department Advisory Board and was an enthusiastic speaker for the Tetley Distinguished Leader Lecture Series, Clary Series, and various commencement and convocation ceremonies. He has served as an advisor to the university's top leadership and helped promote engagement with and among alumni of KSU's graduate programs. In 2016, we inducted him into the Coles College Hall of Fame in recognition of the remarkable path he paved in business and industry.

But the thing that he enjoyed the most was serving as an executive in residence for Coles College because it gave him the opportunity to regularly engage with undergraduate and graduate students. To know Lee is also to know his deep commitment to cultivating the next generation of leaders. He is especially intentional about paving the way for women. This may be because of the deep and lasting influence of what he calls "the Evelyns in my life." His mother, Evelyn, was a fierce and passionate advocate for education, and his wife, Evelyn, is a quiet but powerful influence. Both women helped shape the person he became and showed him that giving someone an opportunity is truly a priceless gift.

I have learned so much from Lee, and one lesson that informs my work each day is the concept of disciplined growth. As an institution, KSU has doubled in size in less than fifteen years. We are now the second largest university in the state of Georgia and show no signs of slowing down. But Lee taught me to see how our mission should drive that growth and urged me to be cautious not to say yes to too much. Our conversations helped me make decisions that are consistent with who we are. He also helped me understand that disciplined growth is related to using the right unit of analysis to make strategic decisions. If we were evaluating a specific program, I welcomed feedback from students, faculty, and alumni, but I needed to look at the program itself. How was it performing? What were the strengths, threats, and opportunities? How does it support our goals? I understood why faculty, staff, and students were passionate about it, but I needed to be rational and evaluate how the program's operations contributed to or veered away from the university mission.

Lee's mentorship has been an extraordinary gift, and I know that I am just one of many that he has influenced. To know Lee is to be changed, and you cannot help but be awed by his story—going from a sharecropper's son to the C-suite. *Soaring* takes you on the journey, and you will see how his eleven guiding principles all derive from his being a value-driven leader. Lee has a powerful moral anchor that guides everything that he does, and his integrity is like the North Star. From him, I learned the importance of articulating my own values and understanding where I was not willing to compromise. This reflection helped me make decisions that align with those values.

Lee has not only made history by becoming the first African American to lead the Lockheed Martin Marietta plant—he also witnessed history being made. When he was fifteen, he was invited to consider early admission at Morehouse College. He remembers being awed by the size of the schools that made up the Atlanta University Center. Even though his sister graduated from Clark Atlanta University, he had never visited. A group of Morehouse students took him on a tour around campus, and they came upon a pickup basketball game and decided to join. Imagine his surprise when he noticed that Dr. Martin Luther King Jr. was playing alongside the boys. He was just a regular guy enjoying an afternoon game, not the larger-than-life icon he had become for so many. They all played for a while, and before King left, he turned and said, "Boys, just remember that hate is too big a burden to bear. It will consume you." Whatever else happened that weekend was eclipsed by that moment, and Lee references it as one of his guiding principles. It helped him survive growing up under Jim Crow, overcome racist incidents while working at a GM subsidiary in Indianapolis, and foster community healing after a mass shooting at a Lockheed plant in Meridian, Mississippi.

I will never forget that story, and I know he never did. He would put those words into practice for the next half century, and he used them to make sense of King's assassination in 1968 and to navigate the struggle for equality and justice in America. Those kinds of experiences change you, but Lee was never driven by bitterness. In fact, these incidents had the opposite effect. They made him more sensitive, empathetic, humble, and willing to dedicate his life and career to making sure that everyone was treated fairly. That is who Lee Rhyant is, and this book tells that story.

Dr. Kathy Schwaig is interim president at Kennesaw State University. Prior to her current role, she served as provost and senior vice president for academic affairs and dean of the Michael J. Coles College of Business at KSU for seven years. Dr. Schwaig is an authority on information privacy and policy formulation.

SOARING

INTRODUCTION

*"Have you lost your
damn mind?"*

O N   M A Y   21, 2018, the *Wall Street Journal* published an article titled, "Where Are All the Black CEOs?" The story goes on to detail the barriers and roadblocks that prevent African American men and women from making it to the C-suite. My unconventional journey from the Jim Crow South to the executive ranks at General Motors, Rolls-Royce Aeronautics, and Lockheed Martin reflects many of these realities. I had a friend tell me once that "a person has a better chance of winning the lottery than ending up in my position from where I came from." I was born in 1950 into poverty in the South after World War II. The fourth of eight children, I was raised by a hardworking African American family of sharecroppers struggling to survive the last decades of segregation. Jim Crow and segregation defined my early life. I was born on the cusp of the civil rights movement, four years before the passage of *Brown v. Board of Education* and five years before the start of the Montgomery bus boycott that helped launch Dr. Martin Luther King Jr.'s career.

How do you get from the Jim Crow South to the top echelons of the aerospace industry? I was inspired by my mother, Evelyn, who had an unshakable belief that I had two advantages over the rest of the world. She used to say that if you are born in this country and you are born to good parents, you can do anything. She also believed in the power of education and read to us every night—from the Bible and the encyclopedia. She pushed us to try new things and be curious. As a result, all eight of the children in my family finished college. I graduated from Lincoln Park Academy in Fort Pierce in 1968 and Bethune-Cookman College in Daytona Beach in 1972. I completed my MBA at Indiana University while working for General Motors and did further study at MIT, Harvard, the General Motors Institute, and the University of Michigan. Most of my brothers and sisters ended up with postgraduate degrees as well. My mother's unrelenting belief in us changed the trajectory of our entire family's future. That lesson was burned into my psyche, and I tried to show the same kind of confidence in my colleagues and employees when I became a leader.

I did not have an easy journey up the corporate ladder, however. I made plenty of mistakes, some bigger than others. One stands out to me even to this day. I joined Detroit Diesel-Allison, a subsidiary of General Motors, in Indianapolis in 1972 after graduating from college. I would stay there, even as the company ownership changed, until I was hired as executive vice president and general manager for the Marietta, Georgia, facility of Lockheed Martin Aeronautics Company in July 2000. In 1984, I was promoted to plant manager at Allison and had more than two thousand people reporting to me. I had just started my MBA at Indiana and had finally made it to top management. That meant that I had arrived on Mahogany Row, the plush office suite with an executive cafeteria that was reserved for the leadership. I was in high cotton and thought I was hot stuff.

One day, I was sitting in my office when Billy Wright, one of my general supervisors, came in without a shirt on and sat down opposite my desk. To say this was unusual is an understatement. There was a strict dress code at the Allison plant, especially for supervisors. We were a shirt-and-tie kind of operation. Billy was not the kind of person you expected to see without his shirt in a professional setting. He was well respected and quite dignified, not to mention a little overweight, clearly well into middle age, and had not seen the sun in some time. This was not a pretty sight. Here he was on Mahogany Row shirtless. What the hell? He started talking about some minor issue that was happening on the shop floor and never even indicated that anything was unusual. I was having trouble concentrating because all I could think was: Have you lost your damn mind? This went on for about ten minutes—a very long ten minutes. I finally had to say, "Billy, what in the world are you doing?" He snapped back, "Do you realize how much you looked like a jackass in the meeting a few days ago? The way you conducted yourself made everyone afraid of you. Now, if people fear you, they are not going to tell you if you have your shirt on or not. They will let you play the fool and sit there like an idiot naked. You do not want to be the kind of leader who doesn't get the truth." All I could think about was the emperor who had no clothes, but Billy was right. When people stop talking to you, you stop being a leader. Leadership is not bullying or dominating, it is about listening. It took a very brave man, one who became a lifelong friend and is now in his mideighties to teach me that. He took a pretty big risk, but it was also a gift, one that I would not soon forget.

Soaring tells my story, my journey, one filled with mistakes, lucky breaks, and mentors who pulled me off a street corner by a shoeshine stand to make sure I made something of myself. It also offers practical leadership and business lessons from my forty years in corporate America. I have distilled those lessons into eleven guiding principles, useful to anyone starting a career, working toward a promotion, or contemplating retirement. My story is not unique. There are plenty of rags-to-riches tales about somebody with modest circumstances making it big. A quick Amazon search or glance at the business section in Barnes and Noble gives you plenty of titles to choose from, a number with Georgia connections. *Time to Get Tough: How Cookies, Coffee, and a Crash Led to Success in Business and Life* tells the story of Michael J. Coles, the cofounder of Great American Cookie Company and the former CEO of Caribou Coffee, who started working at the age of thirteen and had many false starts and painful defeats. *Breaking Ground: My Life in Medicine* is the biography of Louis Sullivan, the first president of the Morehouse School of Medicine and former secretary of the U.S. Department of

Health and Human Services under President George H. W. Bush. Sullivan, who rose out of the Jim Crow South into the world of medicine, is an American success story. Colin Powell recounts compelling stories spanning his teenage years as an ROTC cadet to his later years, when he became secretary of state under President George W. Bush, in his 2012 book, *It Worked for Me: In Life and Leadership*. Bernie Marcus and Arthur Blank tell how they started Home Depot with practically nothing in *Built from Scratch: How a Couple of Regular Guys Grew the Home Depot from Nothing to $30 Billion*.

As with all of these books, *Soaring* combines compelling storytelling with practical lessons to demonstrate the transformative power of perseverance and resilience. What I learned about growing up in the segregated South, working at an early age, graduating from both Bethune-Cookman College and Indiana University, and holding leadership roles in some of the nation's most respected companies also reveals a great deal about the economic, business, and racial climate in the South in the last quarter of the twentieth century.

I end the book with a final chapter that details eleven principles that have helped guide my life and career and that can help you too:

- GUIDING PRINCIPLE 1. Your past does not define your present.
- GUIDING PRINCIPLE 2. You are expendable and replaceable, so constantly update your skills on the job.
- GUIDING PRINCIPLE 3. Do not let anyone tell you where you belong.
- GUIDING PRINCIPLE 4. Do not hate the person but rather the hate inside that person.
- GUIDING PRINCIPLE 5. The most important part of your education happens outside the classroom.
- GUIDING PRINCIPLE 6. Mentors can save your life, and you will need different kinds of support at different stages of your career.
- GUIDING PRINCIPLE 7. Providing someone with an opportunity is a priceless gift.
- GUIDING PRINCIPLE 8. Gifts come from unexpected places.

- GUIDING PRINCIPLE 9. Know what you do not know.
- GUIDING PRINCIPLE 10. Shame never breeds loyalty.
- GUIDING PRINCIPLE 11. Your assets go home at night.

My story echoes the lives of so many others who had great teachers and parents, strong support systems, and the opportunity to get a good education and thrive in a competitive, ever-changing industry. I hope what I have learned on my journey from sharecropper's son to C-suite executive gives you the insight and courage to see how cultivating strong relationships, managing risk, constantly retooling, and giving back to your community can help you live your best life.

I will close with a story about Colonel Bob Brown. He and I worked together at Detroit Diesel-Allison, and he invited my wife, Evelyn, and me to his daughter's wedding. Now, this was a big deal in the 1980s. He was white, and I was black. The reception was hosted by Ulen Country Club in Lebanon, Indiana, founded in 1924 by Henry Ulen. This was a private, member-owned club, not known for its diverse membership in this era. A few weeks before the wedding, one of my friends at the plant pulled me aside and said, "Lee, do not be surprised if Bob does not invite you because this club is only for whites." I was glad for the information, but the next day, I received a personal invitation and warmly accepted. Bob was a good friend, and we were delighted to celebrate this happy occasion with his family. From the moment we were invited until we drove home from that reception that Saturday night, there was not a single moment when Bob or any member of his family made us feel uncomfortable. He never hinted that there would be any kind of issue, and the event was wonderful. But it was not lost on me that Bob was willing to take a pretty big risk in inviting us. He wanted us there and was not going to let restrictive membership policies or intolerance stand in his way. After the event, my friend Tim Ross came up to me and said, "Lee, I hope you would never question Bob Brown's respect for you and your family." I did not, and I was deeply moved that he would be willing to do the right thing at the risk of losing his social capital. That invitation was a gift, and I have been on the receiving end of so many gifts in my life. I hope that in some small way this book and the lessons embedded within it reflects my appreciation for what I have been given. It is also my hope that this book inspires you to look at your own story in new and unconventional ways and, in turn, helps you soar as I have.

CHAPTER 1
YOU HAVE TO ANSWER TO ME

"You have to put in $1.25
worth of effort for a
dollar's worth of pay."

MY GRANDPARENTS, Fred and Amanda Rhyant, and their five
children (Harding, Thomas, Ezekiel, Sid, Mero) left Alabama
during World War II to move to Sasser, Georgia. My father's
family had been slaves in Eufaula and survived Reconstruction and
the era of Jim Crow. Sasser was a little more than fifty miles away,
literally across the lake from Eufaula. Even though my family had
deep roots in Alabama, it was still a dangerous place for African
Americans. The largest city in Barbour County, Eufaula is located
on the Chattahoochee River, and was originally part of Creek Indian territory. The city's wealth grew from the cotton trade and its
location as a shipping center prior to the Civil War. During Reconstruction, cotton shipping resumed, and Alabama was placed in the
Third Military District. In 1874, the White League, a paramilitary
group hoping to regain political power, instigated an election riot
that killed seven African American Republicans, injured seventy,
and drove more than one thousand from the polls. By the turn of
the century, the Democratic-dominated Alabama state legislature,
following Mississippi's lead, passed a new constitution that disenfranchised most blacks through poll taxes, literacy tests, grandfather
clauses, and white primaries. This was just one of the many forms of
intimidation that African American families like mine endured.

Historian David E. Alsobrook explained what life was like in this small town in his book *Southside: Eufaula's Cotton Mill Village and Its People, 1890–1945*, "'Jim Crow' in Eufaula rested solidly upon one basic premise—the lowliest, poorest white farmer, laborer, and cotton mill operator was racially superior to any African-American." Lynchings were common: more than three hundred African Americans were killed by vigilantes in Alabama between 1877 and 1950. In one particularly brutal example, dating from February 1911, Iver Peterson, an eighteen-year-old boy, was murdered by twenty prominent citizens eight miles from Eufaula's city limits. The *Dothan Eagle* reported that "his body was strung up to a limb and riddled with bullets. The body was left hanging there." Many local leaders, including William Jelks, who edited the town newspaper and would later serve as Alabama's governor, were outspoken advocates for white supremacy and promoted lynching as a way of controlling the black population.

Eufaula's history explains, in part, why my family left. But I had a childlike understanding of the move. When I was a boy listening to my uncle Thomas describe the story of the journey, I imagined it to be a thousand miles away, filled with dangers and adventures. I was amused to find out later that it was only fifty-four miles, but I suppose when you are on a mule with all your worldly possessions, it must feel like an eternity.

My family had been sharecroppers since the end of the Civil War, and like so many other black families in the Deep South, worked in the cotton fields in Eufaula and later in Sasser. This was a brutal system that developed throughout the South after Reconstruction and lasted well into the twentieth century. As the *New Georgia Encyclopedia* reported, by the 1880s, 32 percent of all farms in rural Georgia were operated by sharecroppers. That number grew to 37 percent by 1910. Laborers like my family worked on land that was owned by others. To survive, they also raised chickens and pigs, maintained large gardens, and canned vegetables and smoked meat. At the end of the season, the workers might be paid a third of the crop. What should have benefited both parties became a labor system that further disenfranchised African Americans and poor whites. Sharecroppers were often expected to buy seeds, fertilizer, tools, shoes, food, and clothing from the owners. Because workers rarely had cash, they were beholden to a punishing credit system and were often defrauded. Most sharecroppers were illiterate and were not given a chance to review the owners' records for accuracy, which further complicated their situations. As a result, most sharecroppers ended up in an endless cycle of debt and regularly moved from farm to farm to try to improve their circumstances. Erskine Caldwell's 1932 novel *Tobacco Road* famously details the plight of white sharecroppers. More recently Douglas Blackmon's 2008 book *Slavery by Another Name: The Re-enslavement of Black People in America from the Civil War to World War II* tells this story, and I see my family's history reflected in those pages.

My family worked on a farm owned by Henry Brim, who was a fairly typical overseer. We lived in a wooden shack that did not have indoor plumbing. We had a well and an outhouse. The shack was heated with a small fireplace, and outside there was a small fenced area for chickens and pigs. I do not recall much about that time because I was so young, but I do remember not liking how my family was treated. I was not able to point to any specific incident, just a tone that was obvious even to a child.

While the desire to improve the family's prospects partially explains the move from Eufaula to Sasser, it was not the whole story. Over the years, various family members tried to piece together what happened from clues, because my grandfather, Fred Rhyant, was never one to explain what happened. I do know that he changed our name from Ryan to Rhyant when the family moved. While researching our family tree years later, I saw the original name "Ryan" in the public records in Terrell County, Georgia. There were always whispered stories and rumors that my grandfather had beaten up a white man who made advances on my grandmother in Eufaula and had to flee. In the Jim Crow South, that would have made a lot of sense because my grandfather was quite a forceful man who fiercely protected his family. The change in our name always reminded me that there were things worth risking your life for. My grandfather was a preacher, businessman, and entrepreneur. Creative and adventurous, he boasted eleven years of education, which was very un-usual for an African American man born in 1895. He loved taking risks and was very good at working deals. He would buy into vari-ous schemes and loan people money, thus profiting from the inter-est. Years later, when I was playing by the shoeshine stand next to the funeral home in Fort Pierce, Florida, where we moved when I was four, Mr. Gibson, the funeral home director, came out to talk to me and said, "Lee Ernest, you know your grandfather is a very smart man. You better hope you are as good with your money as he is with his." I later learned that my grandfather was an important part of our neighborhood economy; he was shrewd, savvy, and smart.

Despite the fact that my grandfather's parents had been enslaved, my grandfather was well read and would often sit down and talk with me after school, offering commentary on history or current events that I was studying. He called me Little Bill, which I never understood, and was always the family patriarch. Everyone obeyed him because they feared him. He knew a lot and was never afraid to show it. My grandmother Amanda Hicks Rhyant, who died when I was seven years old, could not have been more different from my grandfather. She was a respected matriarch who was also very nur-turing and had a way of speaking her mind. I was close to her be-cause we spent so much time together. My grandfather was the family's financial anchor, but she was the glue that held the fam-ily together. I recall feeling betrayed when she died and can still see the specter of her funeral in 1957. African American funerals in this era were very long, traditional, and dramatic—especially viewed through the eyes of a small child. It was my first funeral, and I had never seen an open casket, nor had I ever seen my father cry. Every-one was wailing and seemed out of control. The whole event trau-matized me, because she was the person I depended on the most, next to my mother, and she was gone. This was my first experience with death—and I learned about its finality and unpredictability.

My father, Harding Rhyant, like most of his siblings, was taken out of school in the fifth grade to work for his family in the cotton fields in Eufaula and later in Sasser. Sharecroppers were "farmers without farms," and more children meant more labor. So it made sense to put children to work as soon as they were able. Our community valued school, but focus on survival came first. My father was very talented and hardworking and spent much of life learning on his own to make up for that loss. He believed that everybody had to earn their own way and would often say, "You have to put in $1.25 worth of effort for a dollar's worth of pay." He was a man of his word, a talented musician, and a deacon in our church, a position he held with great pride. He did not believe any job was beneath him as long as it was performed with dignity and it provided for his family. He had an enduring belief in the power of the vote, having grown up under Jim Crow, and always believed that anybody who failed to try to exercise their constitutional rights was either a coward or lazy, or both. I remember waiting for him on election day, and he would come out of the voting booth with his chest out and head held high. I always thought my father was the eldest of the children, but I later found out that my grandparents had another son, Fred Jr., who was older than my father. He died young, and I never knew him.

My father met my mother, Evelyn Toombs, soon after his family moved to Sasser; he was twenty and she was about eighteen. Her parents had died when she was young, and her brother Peter helped raise her and her brother Bennie. My parents married in 1945 and endured a number of difficult years in south Georgia. When I was four years old, my mother sold her wedding ring and used that money plus the paltry savings she and my father had cobbled together to move the family to Fort Pierce, Florida, to follow my uncle Thomas. He had painted such a rosy picture of the Sunshine State that we were all excited. What we expected to be our Mecca was no Mecca. It was just more hard work. Fort Pierce was incorporated in 1901 and is the county seat of St. Lucie County. Situated along the Indian River, it is about fifty-five miles from West Palm Beach. The fort was established between 1838 and 1842 during the Seminole Wars and was named for the brother of President Franklin Pierce, Lieutenant Colonel Benjamin K. Pierce. A small fishing village grew up around the fort, and it became a center for migrant farms, and that is where my parents ended up, in a migrant camp. It was not much better than Sasser, but we did have more freedom.

Fort Pierce was where noted Harlem Renaissance writer Zora Neale Hurston made her home from 1957 until her death in 1960. In her article "Florida's Migrant Farm Labor," published in *Frontiers*, Hurston wrote about the people who poured into the state with "empty-pockets and high hopes." She goes on to explain that African American families make up the bulk of the labor pool, and she calls them "rushians," for rushing down from Georgia. Hurston quotes one woman who invited the migrants south, "Come down here to get away from Georgia's backside." And that is just what we did.

The move to Fort Pierce was an ordeal; it was 420 miles away and it got hotter and hotter the further south we went. We piled the whole family in an old car and barely made it. This was the height of Jim Crow, so we could not stop at restaurants, restrooms, or hotels. But my mother, Evelyn, was determined that we try something new. She saw that most African American students in the small Georgia towns of Sasser and Albany were dropping out of school, so she turned her attention to Florida, hoping it might offer better opportunities for her children. Almost immediately, it was clear that we were going to have to do migrant work, and I remember living in nothing more than a wooden shack with two rooms until I was about seven. My mother's goal was to find indoor work, and after a few years, she and my father were hired as janitors at Fort Pierce Elementary School.

This was a huge change—they were out of the hot sun and enjoyed their work. Most importantly, they now had steady paychecks that did not depend on the weather or crop yields. The jobs really opened their eyes; they saw firsthand the difference between black and white schools in the Jim Crow South. They were separate but in no ways equal. The black schools were smaller, poorly maintained, and had far fewer resources for students and teachers. A number of people helped my family. Mrs. Garrett at the school always found ways for my parents to work special events off campus to make some extra money. She helped my father start his lawn business. My father did lawn care for numerous white families, and I recall that I used to go along in the summer to help him. One of the women, Mrs. Patasek, would often drive us home after cutting the grass, and we typically rode in the back seat. One day, I was working by my-self, and she invited me to sit in the passenger seat—that was the first time in my life I had ever been in the front seat with a white person. I can still remember the moment she held the door for me. My mother also cleaned houses for Mrs. Meade and Mrs. Collins, and those jobs and the relationships that my parents developed with white women gave them a broader sense of what was possible.

My parents were a major influence on my early life, just as my grandparents had been. My father worked constantly—as a share-cropper in Alabama and Georgia and then as a janitor, bank handy-man, and later as the owner of a small lawn business in Florida. I think that because he never finished his education, he was forced to work hard. He prided himself in never having to ask for help to support his family. He always earned his way, and his word was his bond. But he was not distant, quite the opposite. He was charming, loving, gregarious, and honest. Once, as we were leaving the A&P grocery store, Dad realized that there was a can of tomatoes in his cart for which he had not paid. He turned around immediately and took it to the cashier. She was surprised and said, "You know, no-body would have noticed." To which he replied, "Lee Ernest would know." What he meant was that it would be a bad example for me. Dad was straight as an arrow.

My mother, Evelyn, was fierce, brilliant, athletic, and compas-sionate. She probably shaped my young life more than anyone else. She believed in accountability, optimism, and resilience. She had aphorisms that she used to say all the time, like "Bad stuff happens to everybody—what matters is how you handle it" and "Life, like the weather, has seasons, and you have to have the right clothes for each." I did not fully understand them as a child, but they started to make more sense to me as I matured. She had a unique way of mak-ing everybody feel good about themselves. She was not one to gos-sip or humiliate anyone. Her father, Benjamin Toombs, had been a carpenter and bricklayer, and he died in 1936 when she was eight. Her mother, Laura Toombs, passed in 1943 when she was fifteen. She and her siblings took over the family farm. Life was hard for an orphaned, teenaged African American girl in South Georgia during the Depression and World War II. She was always very sensitive about my peers who lost their parents and urged me to stand in the "gap" to help them.

My mother realized that education was the best path to help us escape poverty. She had to leave school in ninth grade to go to work and never had a chance to go to college. When we moved to Florida she worked as a janitor and cleaned houses to save enough money to go to night school at Indian River Junior College when it desegregated in the 1960s to get her GED. She eventually became a nurse's aide in the local hospital and then an operating room technician (one of three black women in Fort Pierce to hold that position). She made sure her children would have every opportunity (and I can report that all of us have college degrees, several with advanced degrees). She had no tolerance for foolishness, especially about school. If any of us failed to complete assignments or showed any disrespect for authority, we were punished. There was no negotiation. I can really only speak about her relationship with me, but she knew me so well that I could not fool her.

I remember an incident in fifth grade when she came to a parent-teacher conference that was part of an open house. I had been sailing along in school and trying not to garner any attention but was not reaching my potential. I did not like my teacher, Ernestine Davis. She was quick to hit us and seemed to enjoy punishments more than teaching. To stay out of her orbit, I decided to do just enough to get by and not draw any attention to myself. My mother listened to the teacher talk about me as an average student without much potential and patiently waited for her to finish. She only asked that the teacher call her if I was going to be punished. We drove home in silence, and I knew I was in trouble. I can still hear her voice: "Lee Ernest, come here. You are fooling that woman. She's a mean lady, and you're doing a pretty good job of hiding your abilities from her. But I know you are four chapters ahead of the class, and you're just skating along. I'm keeping an eye on your butt. I expect you to finish that book and plenty more before you reach sixth grade. You may fool her, but you have to answer to me." I remember that year as being especially difficult. We struggled financially, my sister Cheryl had been born, and my mother was already expecting another baby.

I attended several schools in Fort Pierce: Means Court Elementary School for kindergarten and part of first grade, Lincoln Park Academy for the rest of first grade through third grade, Frances K. Sweet Elementary for part of third and fourth grade, Chester A. Moore Elementary for fifth and sixth grade, and then Lincoln Park Academy again for seventh through twelfth grade. The move from fifth to sixth grade was transformative. I left Mrs. Davis behind and walked into Charles Hines's classroom and found myself challenged academically for the first time in my life. I was not the smartest kid in the room but joined a group of gifted young students like Ronald Young, Danellena Brooks, Robert Earl Gilchrist, Calvin Henderson, Eddie Evans, and Shirley Platt. My mother saw this as an opportunity and stayed in close contact with Mr. Hines, and he was exactly the kind of teacher you wanted—fair, tough, and never one to shy away from some friendly competition. There was no fooling him, but mostly I did not want to. I was just happy to be in a classroom guided by a talented teacher who was going to push us to reach our potential. At the end of that year, the school district accused Mr. Hines of cheating because his sixth-grade class's standardized test scores were so high. They assumed a group of African American students could not reach that kind of achievement, but they were wrong. Mr. Hines was also my Boy Scouts troop leader, so he had a tremendous amount of influence on me.

Apart from home, work, the shoeshine stand, and school, I spent most of my time as a boy and teenager at Mt. Moriah Primitive Baptist Church. The church was important to my parents, both spiritually and socially. It was founded in 1911 and was part of a nineteenth-century movement that rejected the missionary efforts in the Baptist Church. My father was a deacon, and my mother was a church elder, positions they held with great honor and dignity. This was the deal with my parents—if the church doors were open, you went or you did not go anywhere else but school all week. You went on Sunday and were extremely disciplined. Earl Little was my Sunday school teacher and choir teacher (he was also the choral director at the high school). Mr. Little was one of the most respected men in town. He was born in Fort Pierce, graduated as valedictorian at Lincoln Park Academy in 1944, served in World War II, and under the GI Bill, attended Hampton University in Virginia before matriculating at Oberlin School of Music. The school district later paid for him to complete his master's degree from the University of Michigan. He taught at Southern University in Baton Rouge before returning to Fort Pierce in 1955 to teach music and serve as choral director. He had a major influence on me and so many students in town.

My parents had eight children: Catheryn, Benny, Harding, Lee Ernest, Virginia, Nancy, Cheryl, and Ricky—the last three were born in Fort Pierce. Harding was closest in age to me, and he used to beat up on me until I turned fourteen. Then I was finally bigger than him, and I beat his butt every day for two months to pay him back for the pain he inflicted on me as a child. We eventually worked it out and became close. I was especially attached to my Uncle Zeke, one of my father's younger brothers, and my cousin Jerry Cooper (nicknamed Profile). Uncle Zeke loved cars, and I would ride around town with him and we would talk and joke around a lot. He could tell me what not to do, and I really listened. Though eighteen years older than me, he had a really young spirit and was a great confidante. There was a place in Fort Pierce called the Step Up; it was a hamburger stand near the shoeshine stand where my friends and I used to hang out after school. When I was in middle school, I was with Jerry and other school friends who were smoking cigarettes, which looked pretty cool to a boy. Zeke saw me and Jerry and simply said, "Don't do that." He was not scolding us or trying to humiliate us; he just did not want us to smoke. I heeded his advice until I was in college but later quit. My mother and father, Charles Hines, Earl Little, Uncle Zeke, and other adults in the community became a loosely organized team that raised me. And I know now that I was a full-time job.

Almost from as early as I can remember, I was a leader, but a terrible follower. This was especially problematic for my parents as they tried to scrape together a living for eight children and keep us all out of trouble. My mother used to tell a story about when I was three. My father had spanked me for some long-forgotten transgression, and I sassed back to him that "I'd be back." He spanked me again, and they put me to bed without supper. When they awoke the next morning, I was outside their bedroom door with a brick in my hand. I was not going to give up. In preschool and kindergarten, I led a mutiny and tried to take over the classroom from the teachers. I think my mother was worried that I had some of my grandfather's personality. I certainly seemed to be headed that way. But I was also smart. I learned to read when I was four, could spell almost anything, and had a large vocabulary for a child. Smart and impertinent was not a great combination for an African American kid in the South.

When I was a preteen, my mom and dad went out of town, and my first cousin Jerry, our friend William Earl Jones (called Gabby), and I took my mother's Ford Country Squire station wagon out for a spin. The three of us decided we could manage this, even though none of us could reach the pedals. Jerry tried to work the accelerator, Gabby was responsible for the brakes, and I did my best to steer. No surprise that we could not coordinate our efforts and found ourselves pulled over by the police. When he stopped laughing, Mr. Ellis, the local police officer who knew our family, gave us a pretty stern lecture and drove the car a block and a half back to the house. I still do not know why he never told my parents what actually happened. We certainly all deserved to be punished, but I think he secretly admired our audacity.

My mother saw both my potential and my propensity for trouble and partnered with Mr. Little and Mr. Hines to help guide me. That worked fairly well in school, church, or a Boy Scouts meeting. Zeke was helpful in monitoring my free time. My mother saw my talents but watched me like a hawk. She would often say, "I don't care what your report card says. Teachers are going to grade you on how well you pass their tests. I know what you can achieve, so don't think you're going to scheme your way out of things." She encouraged me to read *Compton's Pictured Encyclopedia and Fact Index* and the classic books that came with the set, such as *Black Beauty* and *Trea-*

sure Island. I read everything I could. She expected me to do extra work and satiate my natural curiosity. She saw my natural leadership abilities but often warned, "Either you do right and reach your potential or do wrong and end up in prison or dead on the street."

My father's work ethic and my mother's unrelenting belief in education composed my first leadership lesson. My parents, along with Uncle Zeke, Mr. Hines, and Mr. Little, showed me that mentors can save your life. None of these people were CEOs. They did not go to business school or read *Forbes* or the *Wall Street Journal*—but their diligence, honesty, and high standards showed me what was possible. They knew what I was capable of and pushed me to try harder and do better. In this way, they put me on the right path. I can still hear their words ringing in my ears, nearly sixty years later. Their example helped shape my future in ways that I would not recognize for many years. They would help me see Ralph Waldo Emerson's wisdom when he said, "The only person you are destined to be is the person you decide to be."

CHAPTER 2
TWO HANDSHAKES

*"You have two advantages over the
rest of the world. If you are born
in this country and you have good
parents, you can do anything."*

MY PARENTS BECAME janitors at Indian River Junior College (founded in 1959 and now Indian River State College) when I was in middle school. In the summers, my brothers Benny and Harding and I helped Mr. Boeing, the man in charge of plant operations, sod the grass in front of the main building. It was really hard work in the hot sun, and we were expected to give the money we earned to our parents. One day, when I was looking for some water, I wandered into the college cafeteria. This was not an integrated school, and as an African American I should not have been in the building and was certainly not permitted to sit down and eat. But I was young and did not know better. Sweaty and dirty, I saw cool water and a plate full of donuts and decided to help myself. Like my father, I was pretty gregarious, never afraid to talk to anyone. So here I am violating every Jim Crow law without even knowing it and having a grand time. This went on for nearly a month. I joked with the cafeteria staff and never realized that some of the white students were paying for my snack. I guess the students and staff saw me as some sort of novelty. I would take a break every day, grab my snack, sit with the white students, and even use the bathroom. My parents and brothers had no idea where I was going. If my mother had found out, she would have jerked a knot in my tail.

One day, while leaving the cafeteria, a young man came up to me and said, "What's your major?" I had no idea what he was talking about, so I said the first thing that popped into my head: "Pete Chavis." I knew that Pete was the school's drum major.

When I saw the confused look on his face, I asked him, "What's your major?" And he replied, "Business." So I said, "That's my major, too."

I knew he was just being nice when he asked me, "What do you want to be?"

I replied, "Martin Luther King said I can be anything I want to be."

He left and came back a few minutes later and gave me a copy of the business section from the *New York Times*. I was really surprised and started reading the business section of papers and magazines. To this day, I wish I could find and thank him. What white college student in the early 1960s would have gone to the trouble to help a poor, young, arrogant, African American boy? He did not seem like he was from the South, but I still believe he was paying for my snacks. I surmise that he also played a role in making sure my parents did not get fired for having such an unruly child. This experience taught me that there was much to learn about race relations and about the wider world. Between reading the encyclopedias and the business sections of newspapers, I was coming to understand that my future was going to be bigger than Fort Pierce.

I look back on this time with fondness but am also stunned by my naivete. Violating Jim Crow laws could get you killed, evidenced by the brutal murder of Emmett Till in Mississippi at age fourteen in 1955 for allegedly offending a white woman in her family's grocery store. Race relations were always complicated under segregation, but my time at the junior college taught me not to be afraid of whites. I would often see the young man from the cafeteria on the campus grounds, and he would always stop and talk to me. I would be planting sod, and we would take a break to just chat. My family was amazed that we seemed to have a real friendship.

I also recall meeting Dr. Maxwell King, the president of the college. When my mother introduced him, he extended his hand to shake mine. That very act—polite physical contact between an educated white man and a black boy with muddy hands—was almost inconceivable. He did not hesitate to give me a firm shake, look me in the eye, and speak to me like an adult. These experiences—one with the white student in the cafeteria and the other with the president—had a big impact on me. I sensed that both of these men had faith in me, and I can still remember the pride I felt in that. That was especially notable in the era of Jim Crow. I had never accepted that I was not as good as any other child, and these interactions seem to prove it.

For seventh grade through graduation, I returned to Lincoln Park Academy, where I had attended school before. The school was founded for African American students in 1906 and garnered a reputation for scholarship, athletics, and student activities. In the 1920s, a survey of schools in Florida, documented on the Florida Stories website, declared: "Education among Negroes in Florida is very spotty, ranging from very good at Lincoln Park Academy, down to the very poorest." Zora Neale Hurston, author of *Their Eyes Were Watching God*, briefly taught there as an English teacher. This was not a separate-but-equal school under Jim Crow that was a poorer version of the local white school. It was an impressive place, so I never felt a sense of inferiority, that I was at the town's "lesser" school. Lincoln Park was accredited and all of the teachers had bachelor's degrees; many had advanced degrees. They were specialists in their fields. As a result, you might have the same social studies or math teacher each year, thus developing a tight bond with them. Mr. Little told me a story years later that, just like with my sixth-grade class with Mr. Hines, the Florida Department of Education reviewed the school's test scores and became suspicious that the students and teachers were cheating. After a thorough investigation, they determined that high-quality teachers and dedicated students explained the exceptional scores.

Many of the graduates of Lincoln Park went on to have distinguished careers, including James Edward Hair, who was among the first thirteen African Americans commissioned officers in the U.S. Navy in 1944, known as the "Golden Thirteen." Invited to the Great

Lakes Training Station near Chicago, the men were kept in a segregated unit and given only eight weeks of training, half of the normal period. Suspecting that they were being sabotaged, the men often stayed up late into the night tutoring each other. When they completed their exams, the navy questioned their scores and had them retested, and the whole group scored even higher (3.89 out of 4). James Hair served as a skipper, then as the first black officer on the USS *Mason* during World War II. After the war, he completed his degree in social work and specialized in foster care and adoption. His story was just one of many, and today Lincoln Park is one of the highest performing magnet schools in the nation.

For a long time, Lincoln Park was the only African American high school from Daytona Beach to Fort Lauderdale, and children came to Fort Pierce from all over the state. They would often board with local families during the week and return home on the weekend. The school, like Mt. Moriah Primitive Baptist Church, was another social center of Fort Pierce. Segregated schools were more than places to learn; they functioned as recreation and community centers for the African American community. Churches played a similar role. Many of the teachers and staff members went to our church, so there was no escaping their scrutiny. Unlike today, teachers were highly respected by the community members. Most of the parents in Fort Pierce, including mine, had dropped out of school early to work in the fields, so their children were often the first generation to graduate high school. A high school diploma was a golden ticket to a better life, so education was valuable, teachers were honored, and graduations were community celebrations. The biggest embarrassment a family could face was to have a child misbehave at school.

I loved high school and thrived, but I recall two incidents with Earl Little, the choir director, that had a profound effect on me. For some reason, he and I got into a heated argument. I am sure he asked me to do something that I refused, so I flipped him off like a fool. When I got home, my mother gave me the choice. She said, "I could force you to apologize, but I want you to spend some time thinking about all the things he has done for you and the children at church and at school. He teaches summer school, brings refresh-

ments to meetings and performances, organizes plays and oper-
ettas, pays for Christmas presents for the children, and is not paid
a penny. He does this out of the goodness of his heart, and you have
the nerve to be disrespectful to him. Think about that." So I did,
and out of sheer appreciation for what he had done, I went back to
school the next day and apologized. That expression of contrition
changed my whole idea about sacrifice. Mr. Little did so much for
me and our community and certainly should not have had to put up
with my bad attitude.

Another incident involved a community performance. Mr. Little
organized an operetta, *The Merry Widow*, with students from Lincoln Park. As we practiced and read through our lines, he would
play one of the characters. One day, he told us he wanted to work
through the first act. We moved pretty quickly and ended up going
into the second act, for which I was not prepared. Boy, did I feel stupid in front of my peers. I was so embarrassed, as only a teenage boy
can be. So I went home and worked all night to learn my entire part.
I came back to school and asked him to quiz me. We read through
the first act again, but he kept reading to see how far I could go.
We made it to the end, and I did not miss a single line. This experience taught me a lot about preparation and personal fortitude. I am
pleased to say that Earl Little is in his nineties and still cuts his own
grass and walks more than three miles a day. We regularly visit and
talk on the phone, and he remembers both of these incidents.

I was in high school when I became interested in Evelyn Ingram,
who would also have a profound influence on the rest of my life. Evelyn was the daughter of Jonathan and Louise Ingram, who were
field-workers. They occasionally traveled around the Southeast as
seasonal workers following the crops. One summer day after finishing my freshman year in high school, I was hanging out at the
shoeshine stand with my friends when Evelyn and her friend Peggy
walked past. I noticed a juicy, red apple in her hand, and I thought
it would be cool to try to take it from her. I did and was making a big
fool out of myself in front of my friends when I felt something hit me
hard on the back of the head. She had thrown a rock at me. When I
lunged at her, she stood her ground. This girl was tough, and I was

impressed. But she mostly ignored me, in the way that teenagers do. Several months into our sophomore year, Jerry told me that Evelyn wanted to talk to me. She was close to my family, especially my mother, and we started dating our sophomore year and became very close. She would also play a critical role in keeping me off the streets and focused on my studies.

I am often asked how I succeeded coming out of the Jim Crow South. There is no easy answer. My mother would say, "You have two advantages over the rest of the world. If you are born in this country and you have good parents, you can do anything." That is true. But I had friends who had similar circumstances, and they did not succeed. Some of them did not survive. I spent a lot of time thinking about what made my story so different. I hung out near the shoeshine stand at Seventeenth Street and Avenue D just like so many boys my age; it gave me a place to go and helped me build community. Some of the young men on the street with me became violent and went to prison—that was not my group. I witnessed some unsavory things, but I always seemed to stay on the periphery. If the guys were planning something, somebody would say, "Lee Ernest, you stay here." I recall one incident when a group of boys from Gifford, Florida, came to jump one of the guys at the shoeshine stand. We knew they were coming and had bats to fend them off. I was leading the charge, but when the police came, my cousin Jerry said, "Lee Ernest wasn't involved." Hell, I was leading the thing, but they protected me. They also took care of our friend Gabby, who was often bullied. Jerry, Godfrey, Clifford, and I all watched over him. We all felt a sense of loyalty because he was one of us.

I remember another time a group of boys was planning to "roll" someone, which usually meant stealing money from somebody who had too much to drink. The man they had targeted was old and lost. Hearing my father's voice in my head about the importance of not taking things that are not yours, I told the boys to leave him alone. Another time, there was an old black man who had hit the numbers (an illegal lottery) and was carrying a lot of cash in his pocket. We knew this because he pulled out a huge wad to pay for his shoeshine. We saw him go into a bar, and boys from another group tried to kick him, but Jerry, Godfrey, Clifford, and I jumped in to stop them. I knew these boys, but I still remember standing up to them when I felt like they had crossed a line. It is amazing that we all survived—this was an era when the police could arrest a black man, woman, or child without even the suspicion of a crime. Being black was enough.

I was no saint, but I also remember being afraid to have to face my mother, my father, the Reverend Bullard at Mt. Moriah, Mr. Hines, Uncle Zeke, and Mr. Little. I also had other activities and responsibilities that competed for my time and attention. Church was a major part of my life. I typed the church bulletin, taught the kids at Sunday school, and went to Vacation Bible School. Choir and extracurricular school activities also kept me off the streets for most of the week. Starting in ninth grade, I was the vice president of my class, and by the time I was in twelfth grade, I was student council president. Dating Evelyn and having close friends like Calvin, Eddie, Jerry, and Gabby in high school also helped keep me in check. These combined influences and activities partly explained why I did not get in too much trouble. But so many of my friends were not so lucky. They got tangled in a web of drugs and incarceration that destroyed them and, just as tragically, their families.

Toward the end of my senior year, I had an experience that helped shape the man I became. In 1968, the teachers at Lincoln Park decided to go on strike at the behest of the Florida Education Association. Their walkout was part of a statewide effort between February and March 1968. The teachers were fighting for more school funding, and it was the first statewide teacher's strike in the United States and was widely supported by the community. To ensure that the students would not suffer, a decision was made to move the seniors from Lincoln Park to the predominately white Dan McCarty High School, named for a former Florida governor. Several years before, African American students had been offered a chance to go to the white school, and while some like my cousin Jerry moved, most stayed at Lincoln Park. On our first day at the new school, the principal had an assembly for all the seniors and invited the student council presidents to come forward. I stood up and so did Carol Strange, the council president at Dan McCarty. We both walked up to the stage, and she politely reached out her hand to shake mine.

Like the handshake I received from Dr. Maxwell King at the junior college years earlier, this was not an incidental gesture. The whole moment could have been awkward and could have gone very differently. So many schools, notably Central High School in Little Rock, Arkansas, had a history of racial violence. But not in Fort Pierce that day. Carol could have refused to touch me or could have simply ignored me, but her generous act set the tone for the next two months. The two groups of students went to class and studied together, and it became clear to the teachers at Dan McCarty that the Lincoln Park students were smart. We did not feel inadequate or like we had been given some prize to attend the white school. We had great teachers and outperformed most of our peers.

The strike was finally settled, and we returned to Lincoln Park, but my attitude toward whites continued to evolve. I knew racism was prevalent, but I started to see that one size did not fit all. I found myself reevaluating my assumptions, questioning what I thought I knew. This awareness led to new insight on effective leadership. It would have been easy to be bitter and angry about growing up under Jim Crow, because there were plenty of indignities that affected my daily life. African Americans faced all kinds of limitations—from where we could eat to whether we could try on clothes in a department store. Our textbooks were beaten up and our teachers were paid less than the white teachers. Morning, noon, and night we had to think about race, and white supremacy could get us killed. We lived and breathed segregation, and much of that struggle was invisible to whites. But the moment Carol took my hand, I started to understand Dr. Martin Luther King Jr.'s dream, when he said that he looked to the day when people "will not be judged by the color of their skin but by the content of their character." Standing on that high school stage in front of my peers—both black and white—I started to see that challenging your assumptions is never a wasted exercise.

The generosity that I witnessed in Carol's handshake, just like what I experienced from Dr. Maxwell years earlier, would set the stage for some powerful leadership lessons that would help shape my future. Their impact was so significant that I spent years trying to track them down. Dr. Maxwell King is in his nineties, and Carol lives about thirty minutes from my home in Georgia. It was important for me to reconnect with them and tell them that I have never forgotten those handshakes. I learned long ago that gifts come from unexpected places, and it is never too late to say thank you.

CHAPTER 3
I HAD TWENTY DOLLARS

"I'm betting my last
twenty dollars on
a sure thing."

A
S PART OF HIS War on Poverty program, President Lyndon B.
Johnson encouraged the creation of youth-based initiatives to
help promote education and employment, especially in minority communities. Johnson unveiled this program during the
State of the Union address on January 8, 1964. The accompanying
legislation was in direct response to a soaring national poverty rate
that reached 19 percent, a problem that directly affected my community. In response to this effort, Fort Pierce created a Neighborhood Youth Corps that worked closely with the local employment office, and I was randomly assigned to work for the H. D. King Power
Plant, which was about two miles from my house at 432 North Six-
teenth Street. From the end of my sophomore year at Lincoln Park
Academy in Fort Pierce, Florida, through my senior year in college
at Bethune-Cookman College in 1972, I worked at the power plant,
an electricity-generating facility for the Fort Pierce Utilities Authority. The downtown facility was located between Second Street and
Indian River Drive (and later demolished in 2008 decades after it
closed). Despite my job not being typical work for an African American teenager in the 1960s, I worked full time in the summers, on the
weekends, and during all of my school breaks. This would prove to
be one of the most important jobs I have ever held.

Looking back, the youth corps was a stroke of genius by President Johnson. Jobs were difficult to come by in impoverished neighborhoods, and this program provided a way for teenagers to earn their own way and kept them occupied during the summer months. The job often provided them with money for school, clothing, and food to help their struggling families. I came to appreciate the structure and high expectations—laziness, poor attendance, and bad attitudes were not tolerated. Their rules echoed those that I had been taught by my parents, and many of the corps' counselors were teachers in our community. Like my peers, I saw the job as a badge of honor. It was certainly better than working in the fields, being bored, or being broke.

Before the youth corps program, I had worked other jobs. As a middle school student, I did landscaping with my brothers at Lincoln Park Junior College. I helped my father cut grass for his landscaping company, and for a short while, I worked at Lewis Grocery Store. I occasionally worked at the funeral home for Mr. Gibson, and it was a blessing not to have to labor in the orange groves and tomato fields like many of my friends. My parents had been sharecroppers, and I did not want to follow that path. One summer, I worked at John Carroll High School (a Catholic school in Fort Pierce) doing general janitorial, landscape, and maintenance work. However, the power plant offered something completely different and would ultimately play a big role in my future.

The plant hired me as a mechanic's helper, and I discovered on my first day that there was only a handful of African American employees: Clayton Grier, Emmett Barnes, and Ernest Ghent. They all had long tenures and were well respected at the plant and in the community. I knew these men. Mr. Ghent attended the same church as my family, Mt. Moriah Primitive Baptist Church, as did Mr. Barnes's brother's family. Clayton Grier's daughter went to Lincoln Park Academy with me. The poise, professionalism, and skill that these three men displayed set an excellent example for me, and although I was certainly young, inexperienced, and nervous, their presence inspired me with a measure of confidence. While I knew

racism was rampant in the South, I saw very little overt expressions
of it at the plant. I think this was because many of the men working there were from the North, and we had great leadership that was
not tolerant of discrimination.

I now see how lucky I was to have these three men help me navigate a complicated new position, and they also helped arrange informal apprenticeships within the plant. They never talked down
to me or treated me as a child; they often found ways to make sure
I received overtime. Even though Clayton was at least twenty years
my senior, we became good friends. He taught me a great deal about
maintenance and what tools and skills were needed to do a wide
range of repairs. Emmett worked with Virgil, a white man who
served as the master mechanic. Virgil could operate every machine
on the premises, and the better he got to know me, the more he
taught me about welding, grinding, and drill press operations. Soon
I could operate every machine in the shop. He was always showing
me new things during lunch or during breaks and seemed to appreciate my interest and willingness to learn. It was Virgil who introduced me to Jimmy (the plant manager) and Jack (his assistant).
I do not recall the circumstances of our meeting, but both men
seemed willing to push me to hone my skills. I was equally amazed
that they insisted that I call them by their first names, an unwritten
violation of Jim Crow laws at this time.

In addition to the regular employees, teams of engineers from
Western Electric were often on site to overhaul the generators or do
other repairs. They came from the North and appeared to have a different view of race relations. When at the power plant, they needed a
gopher, and I believe that Jack and Jimmy put me forward. This was
auspicious, because the engineers took me everywhere and taught
me various elements of the overhaul program. They also showed me
how to read blueprints, gave me books, and explained the theories
behind how things worked—skills that would serve me well when I
would later work for General Motors, Rolls-Royce, and Lockheed
Martin. Many of these engineers knew that my family was hardworking but struggling, so they made sure I had plenty of work that
was well compensated. They knew I planned to go to college and

wanted to help me earn enough money to make that possible. By the end of the summer of my senior year of high school, I had saved enough money to help buy new school clothes for my younger siblings and help my parents offset some household expenses. My goal was to be independent but also to continue to help my family. My job at the power plant allowed me to do that and so much more.

As my high school graduation approached in the spring of 1968, I found myself in a world of turmoil. The aforementioned teachers' strike in Florida resulted in our school being temporarily merged with the local white high school, an unsettling experience for everyone, but one we weathered. But that was a small concern in the face of the war, protests, and uncertainty that seemed to be raging around us. The Vietnam War was in full force, and I had to register with the Selective Service in the spring because my eighteenth birthday was fast approaching. As a result, I ended up with a draft number in the middle of the pack—116. That was not much comfort and left me with two choices—go to college or go to war. Many young men of my generation found themselves in the same situation. This was an uncertain time, and the launch of the Tet Offensive by North Vietnamese communist troops in January 1968 prompted widespread antiwar protests on and off college campuses.

Then, on April 4, 1968, the world turned upside down. James Earl Ray gunned down Dr. Martin Luther King Jr. on the balcony of the Lorraine Motel in Memphis. Dr. King had been my hero, and the hero to so many in our community. I met him briefly two years earlier at an informal pickup basketball game that he was playing with some kids near Morehouse. I visited the college my sophomore year of high school and was invited to enroll in my junior year—something we considered to ensure that I could further my education. My mother and I made the trip to Atlanta, and several Morehouse students gave me a tour of campus. We stumbled on a court and saw King playing with a group of boys. They came in contact with him often, but I had only read about him and seen him speak. I was awestruck and expected him to be seven feet tall with a cape. He was my hero, but watching him that day on the court and having a chance to meet him made him all the more real to me.

For many years, King led the charge for change and brought a kind of leadership to the civil rights movement that kept it on the front pages of the newspaper. Now he was gone. In the aftermath of the assassination, the nation erupted into riots. Washington, D.C., Chicago, Baltimore, Detroit, Pittsburgh, Trenton, Wilmington, Louisville, Kansas City, Cincinnati, city by city, block by block, everyone seemed to be on fire. In total, more than one hundred cities erupted, leaving 39 people dead, more than 2,600 injured, and 21,000 arrested. These riots came on the heels of Vietnam War protests that had already heightened tensions in numerous communities.

Major riots made the front pages in the major newspapers, and Florida cities like Tallahassee, Gainesville, Fort Pierce, Tampa, and Jacksonville reported street demonstrations, arson, and fire bombings. I remember on the day and evening after the murder that downtown was flooded with protestors and police in full riot gear with dogs. A number of the police officers said things like: "Why are you all so upset? He was just a rabble-rouser and got what was coming to him." That, more than anything, infuriated the African American mourners, and I remember storming home and finding my mother panicked about my whereabouts. She grabbed me and made me put my head in her lap, asking me to slow down and consider, "What would Martin do?" Once I calmed down, she said, "Look, we've lost Martin, and I just can't lose you, too." With the war in Vietnam and now the assassination, so many black men of my generation started to feel that they had nothing to lose. I know now that my mother was trying to protect me from myself. I believe some of the Fort Pierce leaders intervened to keep the police from further escalating the situation.

The Florida Memory project, sponsored by the State Library and Archives of Florida, has documented many similar events around the state, including the death of Travis Crow, who died when his family's grocery store was bombed in Tallahassee in 1968. Governor Claude Kirk tried to calm tensions, working with local sheriffs and police departments to avoid further violence. In honor of Dr. King, he insisted that all flags on public buildings be flown half-mast for two days and issued a press release calling for nonviolence. Horse and dog racing were suspended, jai alai games were postponed, and a number of labor unions called for a daylong work stoppage. George Gore, the president of Florida A&M University, closed the school for a weeklong "cooling off period," and the NAACP urged Floridians to use April 9, the day of King's funeral, for a period of "sober reflection" instead of protest.

The postassassination riots created the greatest wave of social unrest our nation had seen since the Civil War. In January 2018, the *Smithsonian* declared 1968 "The Year That Shattered America," and having lived through it, I would agree. The article presents a month-by-month timeline detailing the tumult. Starting in January with the Tet Offensive, the article presents a litany of unrest: the stalemate in Vietnam; student protests on multiple college campuses, including New York University, Howard University, and Columbia University; a shootout between Black Panthers and Oakland police; the assassination of Robert F. Kennedy in Los Angeles; violence at the Democratic National Convention in Chicago; and protests at the Olympic Games in Mexico City by Americans Tommie Smith and John Carlos after receiving medals in the two-hundred-meter dash.

It was as if the world had erupted, and here I was an eighteen-year-old African American boy graduating from high school and trying to figure out what to do next. I had been seriously looking at colleges and had a number of acceptance letters from historically black universities such as Morehouse in Atlanta, Howard University in Washington, D.C., and Hampton University in Virginia. As student council president at Lincoln Park Academy, I had given a graduation speech in May of that year that was published in the *Fort Pierce News Tribune*. I heard that some white community leaders, whom I had known through my parents and my work at the power plant, sent the speech to Oberlin, the University of Michigan, and the Air Force Academy, because those institutions were soon contacting me as well. I ultimately received ten offers but chose Bethune-Cookman College in Daytona, about 130 miles from Fort Pierce. My brother Benny was a student there, so I knew the campus. They offered me a generous academic and vocal scholarship, which made it even more appealing. Because I was still worried about the draft, I did not want to stray too far from home and the two Evelyns in my life, my mother and girlfriend. If I stayed nearby, I could also continue to work at the power plant. So in August 1968, I moved to Daytona to start the next chapter in my life.

Bethune-Cookman College was established in 1923 as a merger between Cookman Institute (established in Jacksonville in 1872) and Daytona Literary and Industrial Training School for Negro Girls (established in Daytona in 1904). In 1931, the college was officially named Bethune-Cookman College to pay homage to the legendary Dr. Mary McLeod Bethune. She was an extraordinary woman, both a noted educator and head of the National Council of Negro Women. She was part of President Franklin Delano Roosevelt's "black cabinet" and lobbied Eleanor Roosevelt to encourage the government to open training programs on the campuses of historically black colleges and universities, which helped start the legendary Tuskegee Airmen. That is just one of her many accomplishments, and I felt a great deal of pride going to a school that had such visionary leadership.

During my tenure at Bethune-Cookman, Dr. Richard V. Moore Sr. served as president and oversaw a significant expansion of academic programs, including new majors in music, physical education, health sciences (including premedicine, dental, and pharmacy programs). He coordinated the construction of sixteen new buildings as well; the Carl Southwick Swisher Library was dedicated during my junior year. Enrollment in the college doubled during Dr. Moore's tenure (1947–1975), and the school counts a number of notable alumni, including civil rights leader A. Philip Randolph, inventor Marjorie Joyner, and football Hall of Famer Larry Little.

At Bethune-Cookman, I elected to major in math and sociology. I felt that my time at Lincoln Park Academy had prepared me well because the faculty members had advanced degrees and were exceptional teachers. In my junior and senior years of high school, I was able to participate in an unofficial dual enrollment program at Lincoln Park Junior College (the segregated version of Indian River Junior College). Mr. Floyd, who attended my church and was the principal of both Lincoln Park Academy and Lincoln Park Junior

College, allowed me to attend, and this gave me college-level credit, particularly in the hard sciences, which proved especially helpful. Add to that everything I learned at the power plant from the engineers who brought me technical manuals and books to study, and I felt equipped for college life.

A number of people influenced me at Bethune-Cookman, just as I had significant mentors in my early years. For my freshman year, I roomed with my brother Benny, Glen Leverette, and Kenneth Brockington, who were all upperclassmen. We had a wild time, and I believe their graduation was the best thing to ever happen to me. Rooming with Clarence George in my sophomore year helped me regain focus and gave me some stability. In my junior year, I moved to an off-campus apartment on Keech Street with Broderick McKinney (from Bradenton, Florida) and George Miller (a Vietnam air force veteran). George was like a big brother to both of us. He was older, had been to war, and was serious about his schoolwork. Like my Uncle Zeke when I was a young teenager, he was an anchor and a confidant. The evening before we were scheduled to leave for the Christmas holiday my junior year, we played cards and ate donuts to celebrate the end of our exams. The next morning, we all drove home. Over the break, we learned that George had been killed in a car accident in Lloyd, Florida, on December 31, 1971, while returning from visiting his grandmother. We were all devastated, and I remember that Charles Wesley Moore, the son of the president of Bethune-Cookman and the assistant football coach, drove us to his funeral. I remember that soon after the accident, the school packed up his personal items and sent them to his family. This was not the first time I had encountered death, but it really shook me. As a teenager, you believe that you are invincible and that nothing can touch or hurt you. I knew from my childhood that this was not true, but it did not take away the sting of losing George.

Broderick and I remained close friends and roommates through the rest of my time at Bethune-Cookman, so close that I would later name one of my twin sons after him. We were an unlikely pair. He was an Alpha Phi Alpha, and I pledged Omega Psi Phi. Alphas were known for being reserved and bookish; Omegas were more outgoing and streetwise. Broderick was active in the student government association, while I was active in choir. We became very close, especially after George's death. Though our housing was set up for three students in our junior year, the landlord allowed the two of us to stay there until May by ourselves after George was killed. He realized how significant the loss was and did not want to complicate things.

This would not be the only loss I experienced in college. A young man from my high school was killed in Vietnam, and his story became national news. On August 8, 1970, a Viet Cong mortar shell exploded and killed Specialist 4 Pondextuer Eugene Williams of Company D, Second Battalion, Seventh Cavalry, First Air Cavalry Division. Gene, as he was known to us, was born in Fort Pierce in 1950, and we were the same age. His family attended Bethel Baptist Church, and we were friends. He was one of the first black students to attend Dan McCarty High School, graduating in 1968, and lettering in football and track. Without the resources to attend college, he joined the army and was shipped to Vietnam in November 1969. That following August, he became the nineteenth young man from our county killed in the war.

His death was terrible, but it became symbolic of the pain of segregation as well when Hillcrest Memorial Gardens refused to allow his burial, despite running advertisements in the *Fort Pierce News-Tribune* that free plots were available in the "veterans Garden of Honor." Historian Robert A. Taylor writes about Williams's story in his article "In the Interests of Justice: The Burial of Pondextuer Eugene Williams" in the *Florida Historical Quarterly* in the winter of 2004. He recounts that Williams's mother refused to bury his body and how the standoff became national and international news. The resulting coverage eventually involved the White House and Justice Department, and President Richard Nixon saw it as an opportunity to promote desegregation in the South as part of his reelection strategy. It is no surprise that this issue cast a negative light on Fort Pierce. Mayor Dennis Summerlin's office received hundreds of letters. Nearly four weeks after his death, a federal court decision on August 27 forced the issue, and a funeral for Williams was held two days later at Hillcrest. This terrible ordeal told my community a painful truth—Jim Crow was not dead, and black soldiers were expected to sacrifice their lives a world away for freedoms they did not enjoy at home. While this small battle for a dignified burial was won, the war against racism would continue to rage.

At Bethune-Cookman, in my freshman year, I befriended a white student, Coryendon "Buzz" Nurse, from Stewart, Florida. Like me, he was recruited by the college's choir director, and he used to call me his "homeboy" because our hometowns were only eighteen miles apart. We often carpooled to campus together, and Buzz was a character. It took a strong personality to be one of the few white students at an all-black school in the late 1960s and early 1970s. I recall many intimate conversations that Buzz and I had about race relations. We talked candidly about racial stereotypes, misconceptions, and taboos, the kind of serious conversations you have with your family or close friends. I also recall that there were regular protests, and some of the members of the more outspoken groups that came onto campus would bother Buzz, but we all stood up for him. The college was like a family; that was a legacy left by Dr. Mary McLeod Bethune. If you bothered one of us, you bothered us all, regardless of your race, ethnicity, or gender.

I remember one occasion when Buzz and I were shopping at a drug store with two fellow female students. It was during the Daytona 500, so the city was teeming with tourists. A rough group of white guys saw us together and started to attack Buzz after accusing him of "race mixing." We were outnumbered and trying to figure out what to do when a group of Bethune-Cookman students walked in and immediately came to our aid. That was the Bethune-Cookman way. Buzz majored in sociology, became a lawyer, and passed away in 1998. We lost touch after graduation, but he was the first close white friend I ever had.

A number of faculty members served as mentors for me during college, including Professor Thomas Demps, the choir director. The choir became my family, and I had practice every day from 5:30 to 7:30 p.m. Demps, a native of Key West, was a Bethune-Cookman graduate and veteran who sang in the 372nd Infantry Regiment Glee Club during World War II. After the war, he returned to campus, pledged Omega Psi Phi fraternity, and finished his degree. He would go on to receive his master's degree in music from Columbia University. For several years, he traveled with the Leonard De Paur Chorus, and he returned to Bethune-Cookman in 1954 to become an instructor of music and choir director. Fondly called "Doc," he took the choir all over the nation, including in 1960 when they sang at Carnegie Hall and in 1971 when they participated in the Jerusalem Festival of American College Choirs. He was bemused by the changes on campus during this period and would look at the students dressed in hippie garb with Afros playing the bongos and just shake his head. He had a wry sense of humor and was able to take a diverse group of young men and women and mold them into a cohesive unit on and off the stage. He used to say, "The ages fourteen through twenty-two seem like a long time, but if you can get through those years without scars that haunt you for the rest of your life, you've struck gold." For many years, I have used the lessons he imparted in class to inspire and build leadership teams, and I was sad to learn of his passing in 1994.

Dr. Otis Watson was another mentor. He taught sociology and business and used to say, "You're in the fifteenth round of the fight with one second left and you're losing. You've got to find a way to knock that sucker out. Equality cannot be wrapped around sorrow, pity, and revenge." He would often give me two grades: the one that I earned, and the one he thought I truly deserved that reflected my potential. He really pushed me. I remember one night we were in town and stopped at a Royal Castle for a hamburger. He insisted on paying for my meal. I was a little embarrassed until he told me to pay the favor forward and help somebody else, a lesson that shaped my philanthropy later in my life. Dr. Charles Cherry was equally influential. He taught in the business school and was the owner and publisher of the *Daytona Times*, a five-term Daytona Beach city commissioner, and longtime president of the Florida NAACP. I believe I took only one course from him, but he always taught about service to the community. Today, the Charles Cherry Community Holiday Festival is named for him. Good friends with Professor Demps, Dr. Cherry was especially helpful to me after George's death. Because I lived off campus, I used to hang out in Professor Demps's office between classes, where I often encountered Dr. Cherry. He was a fellow Omega and was the advisor for my fraternity. Though I had only one class with him, he had an outsized impact on my life and became an informal counselor at a time when I really needed it. To this day I remember and cherish his advice, "Surround yourself with people who will tell you the truth in a way that you can hear them without getting mad."

Throughout my time in college, I was singularly focused on my education. My girlfriend, Evelyn, was a year behind me in school and stayed at Lincoln Park Academy to finish her senior year. We spent a lot of time on the phone, and during Christmas and spring break we tried to spend as much time together as possible. But that was difficult, because I was working at the power plant and she was busy with school and her family. Evelyn applied to a number of colleges and finally chose Florida A&M (known as FAMU) in Tallahassee. It was her decision, and I did not want to influence her. She received a scholarship that helped pay for her first year and worked at the student union, library, and in the tomato fields to save extra money. She majored in elementary education and managed to save enough money to make her own way. She was one of seventeen children, and her parents did not have extra money to help her. In retrospect, it was a good decision for us to attend different colleges—it helped us appreciate the time we were together.

By the end of my sophomore year, I was convinced that Evelyn was the person I wanted to marry. We continued to date and visit each other over the next several years, but when I left Fort Pierce in December 1971 after a big fight, I was convinced that our relationship was over. The day after I returned to campus, Broderick called to tell me that Evelyn was in Daytona. I was stunned—certain that she never wanted to see me again. I later learned that she had gotten off the bus on her way back to Tallahassee and came to patch things up. To this day, I am convinced that if she had stayed on that bus, our lives would have been completely different. We both went back to school, and I worked hard to finish the final semester of my senior year.

During spring break, I received some unexpected news from Evelyn saying she was pregnant. I had known for some time that we were going to get married, but we both wanted to finish school first. During this time, our parents played a critical role in supporting us in our decision. With the added pressure of parenthood, I threw myself into my studies and job search. A number of companies sought to recruit a more diverse workforce in the 1970s and turned their attention to historically black colleges and universities. Though not officially scheduled to interview that day, I ran into Wes Eckler, a General Motors executive, outside a career fair. We started talking, and he asked me about my classes at Bethune-Cookman and my work history. We discussed the power plant, and I could tell he was surprised to hear me talk with some expertise about gas turbine engines. I had real work experience, had excellent technical skills, was comfortable talking with some authority with whites, and did not have a southern accent. After about twenty minutes, he asked me how quickly I could change into interview clothes. I ran back to my apartment, put on a suit and tie, and raced back to campus in time to participate in a number of interviews that afternoon. I must have done well, because I was invited to eight onsite interviews at General Motors plants and subsidiaries in Anderson, Newcastle, and Indianapolis in Indiana and in Detroit and Grand Rapids in Michigan in March. The company made me five offers, and I chose to work in the Indianapolis plant because Wes had so much faith in me, and I would be a little closer to home. By April, I had a job, was poised to graduate, and was about to become a father.

I focused my last month in college on my final exams, and three days before graduation, I participated in a senior trip to DeLand, Florida. While I was gone, somebody broke into our apartment and stole most of my clothes. I was not too worried about my casual things, but they took my suits, so I no longer had anything to wear to my new job. When I came back home to Fort Pierce after graduation, I told my mother what happened. For the next few months, my parents and I all worked extra jobs to help raise enough funds to buy appropriate work attire, an iron, and some other things I would need to start my new job. I helped my father with his landscaping business, and my mother took extra shifts at the hospital. Late in the spring, Evelyn and I decided to say our wedding vows with the Reverend Bullard presiding. It was a modest affair, with my parents at our side. This helped give me confidence that Evelyn would be cared for while I made the move to Indiana.

On the drive to Melbourne to catch the flight to Indianapolis, my mother gave me an envelope stuffed with one-dollar bills and change. She had already done so much to help me prepare for this next step that I felt I could not take anything else and said: "Keep your money, Mama. I can manage." She turned to me and with the fierce gaze I had come to know so well, she snapped, "I have been giving to you my whole life, and don't you think I'm going to stop now. I'm betting my last twenty dollars on a sure thing." She had the confidence that she had raised me to do the right thing, and it was now my turn to prove that I could.

That twenty-dollar gift and what it represented is still seared in my brain. It launched me, but it also reminded me that you stand on the shoulders of those who raise and mentor you. On December 8, 2012, I was invited to return to Bethune-Cookman to deliver the commencement address. I closed my talk by telling the graduates that I had put twenty dollars in every diploma. My mother had faith in me as a college graduate, and I wanted to convey to this talented group of young men and women that I had the same kind of faith in them. When I go back to campus, I still meet students who tell me that they framed the money, and that their parents told them to never spend it. My small gift was a big story until Robert F. Smith promised Morehouse College students in Atlanta that he would pledge a gift to the university to pay off every student loan for the 2019 graduating class. Whether you give twenty dollars or thirty million dollars, having faith in those around you is a lesson that can change your life.

CHAPTER 4
HOW WILL THEY KNOW YOU?

*"What will you say and do to
show that you are responsible,
respectable, diligent, and worth
somebody's investment?"*

THOUGH EXCITED ABOUT my new job with General Motors, I
was moving to a city where I knew no one. I did not have a car. I
had no experience living outside of the South, and I barely had
enough money to pay for a few meals. I walked off that airplane in
Indianapolis in June 1972 and remember being scared to death. I
had no idea what to expect, having never lived in the Midwest. However, I soon learned that racism was not confined to the South, and
that there are good people everywhere. Indiana had a troubled racial
history, and those problems would shape my perceptions of my new
home and job. I would have to draw on the lessons I learned from
my parents and mentors in Fort Pierce and at Bethune-Cookman
to survive.

If you asked the average person where racism was most entrenched in the United States, they would likely say the South. But
that does not tell the whole story. The Midwest, like much of the nation, has a long and troubled history, and Indiana was in some ways
an epicenter. D. C. Stephenson, appointed grand dragon of the Ku
Klux Klan in Indiana in 1923, once declared, "I am the law in Indiana." Historian Leonard J. Moore noted that 22 percent of the white
men living in Vanderburgh County (160 miles southwest of Indianapolis) were proud members of the KKK in the 1920s, and the
group would participate in local parades well into the 1980s. I soon

learned that I would be living only forty-four miles from Martinsville, an alleged Ku Klux Klan stronghold that was also known as a
"sundown town," where African Americans were not welcome after dark. On September 16, 1968, just four years before I walked off
that plane, Martinsville became infamous for the brutal murder of
Carol Jenkins, a young black woman stabbed to death while selling
encyclopedias.

That case was terrifying and a deep blow to African American
communities throughout Indiana. Jenkins was born in Franklin,
graduated from Rushville High School, and went to work for the
Philco Division of Ford Motor Company. When a strike shut the
plant down, she took a job as a door-to-door encyclopedia sales-
person. Dressed in a white turtleneck, olive green wool pants, and
a brown jacket with a bright yellow scarf, she volunteered to go to
Martinsville, about twenty-five miles away, with three of her coworkers. In Martinsville, she reported that as she walked, two white
men began following her in a car, screaming racial slurs at her. She
asked a white couple that she saw on the street, Don and Norma
Neal, for help, and they called the police. The police came to the Ne-
als' home, took a statement, and later found the two men who ad-
mitted to following her. After the police left, Norma Neal walked
with Carol for a few blocks to help her find her coworkers but eventually left Carol to continue walking to the prearranged rendezvous
point. About half an hour later, the two men chased Carol down,
held her arms, and stabbed her with a screwdriver. After the murder, Carol's father asked the local police to bring in the FBI but they
refused, and the case remained unsolved. I was only two years older
than Carol, and this was the world that I stepped into.

By the time I arrived in Indiana, Martinsville had become infamous, and Indianapolis was not much better. While the 1954 Su-
preme Court decision *Brown v. Board of Education* formally signaled the beginning of school desegregation nationally, the Indiana
General Assembly passed a law to integrate the schools five years
earlier. But Indianapolis was particularly resistant to the change. In
1968, the year I started college at Bethune-Cookman, the U.S. Department of Justice filed a series of lawsuits against the Indianapolis

Public Schools (IPS) alleging continued discrimination. When the city agreed to merge its public services with Marion County in 1970, under a plan dubbed Unigov, the school systems were excluded, thus creating eleven separate school districts, further isolating African American students. One year later, in August 1971, IPS was ordered to expedite its desegregation efforts.

Other cities had followed a similar model to simplify city services and grow the tax base, but Indianapolis was the only city to refuse to include the school system in the change. Mayor Richard Lugar explained in a 2016 article in the *Atlantic* by Shaina Cavazos that: "Unigov was not a perfect consolidation. A good number of people really wanted to keep at least their particular school segregated." Harmon Baldwin, who served as superintendent of Wayne Township in the 1960s, further argued, "There were other factors that were more important to the residents of the suburban areas than race. If you live in the rural areas, you are suspicious of what's happening in the city area. They were proud of their individual high schools." Landrum Shields, the first black president of the Indianapolis School Board in 1967, countered in the book *Governing Metropolitan Indianapolis: The Politics of Unigov*, by C. James Owen and York Willbern, that Unigov ensured the continued segregation of black students, even after busing was ordered between districts in 1979.

Unigov did have some positive effects on the city. The decades after the merger in 1970, Indianapolis grew in size and stature, and the merger boosted the city's economic power. General Motors, the company that had just hired me, profited directly from this change. But the school system continued to falter; shrinking from 108,743 students in 1967 to 57,000 by 1981. Butler University history professor Emma Lou Thornbrough wrote in her 1993 manuscript "The Indianapolis Story": "If the General Assembly had not exempted the suburban school corporations in enacting the Uni-Gov law, the State of Indiana would not have been found guilty of (intentional) segregation."

It was unsettling to learn this history, but I was also optimistic because I was going to work for General Motors, one of the nation's most respected companies. The division that hired me in the 1970s, Detroit Diesel-Allison, was the result of a merger of two companies: Detroit Diesel and Allison Gas Turbine. Detroit Diesel was founded in 1938 by General Motors. In the early years, it produced the two-cycle Series 71 engine widely used for construction, military, and standby generators. Those engines were also installed in buses manufactured by Yellow Coach (a company that GM acquired in 1943). By the 1950s, the company had developed heavy-duty engines, like the Series 53, for commercial trucking. The second company was founded by industrialist James A. Allison, who established Allison Speedway Team Company to produce race car components in 1915. It was later renamed Allison Engineering Company. The company was purchased by Eddie Rickenbacker in 1927, then Fred and Carl Fisher (who had founded Concentrated Acetylene Company), who ultimately sold it to General Motors in 1929. The company designed dozens of engines—such as the J-35, T-40, T-56, T-63, AE-2100, and the AE-007 (all designed in Indianapolis). The company's most successful engine—the Model 250 turboshaft-turboprop engine—was manufactured starting in the 1960s when helicopters began being powered by turbines. The Bell 206 Jet Ranger and Long Ranger helicopters and the Sikorsky S-76 helicopter all used Allison engines. In 1970, Allison merged with Detroit Diesel to become Detroit Diesel-Allison Division. In 1983, the gas turbine operations, where I worked, separated from this division as Allison Gas Turbine under Dr. F. Blake Wallace. The company's products were excellent, and the motto—"Our power is our people"—was true. Even after I left the company to move to Lockheed, we used Allison's T-56 and AE-2100 in the C130 airplane.

This was a big company, and I found myself at the age of twenty-two as a salaried employee with a big job to do. I knew that I could not fail; Evelyn and my soon-to-be-born child were counting on me. As I prepared for my first day at GM, I remember thinking about something my mother would ask me. When she was trying to get me to reflect on my behavior or reputation, she would ask: "How will they know you?" She really meant: "What will you say and do to show that you are responsible, respectable, diligent, and worth somebody's investment?" A few nights before I left, I was in the kitchen helping her cook, and she told me: "Lee, when I'm working, I never slack off or make excuses. I put my supplies in a certain order and keep my work area clean. I make sure that I am careful and always double-check my work to avoid careless errors. These small things tell people who I am. You have to do the same and let everyone know who you are so they will want to keep you." In a more modern context, she was really asking me: "What is your brand?" I gave her question some thought that night and decided that I would show up early every day, take short lunches, and come back early from breaks. I would not be absent and would make it a point not to gossip or complain on the job. With this plan, I prepared myself for my first day.

General Motors was very helpful and supportive in the transition. For the first two weeks, they put new hires up at the Holiday Inn and provided a per diem. While there, I met other recent college graduates from the South. Adrien Jackson (A.J.) and Marion Sylvester were from the Tuskegee Institute, and Jack Bird had come from Atlanta after finishing at Morris Brown. We all became good friends, and I was especially grateful that A.J. had a car. I was hoping to buy one, but he said he would happily drive me around so I could save money. To this day, I still do not know what I did to deserve such a loyal friend. He was from Tuskegee in Alabama, and I was from Bethune-Cookman in Florida. From the first day we met, he treated me like a brother—and became one of my closest friends. In the evenings after work, we drove around town to explore the city. I think we both expected that because we were in a large metropolitan area in the Midwest that we would enjoy more enlightened views on race relations. On the few occasions that we ventured beyond the city limits, we would find ourselves in sundown towns, and our very presence was unsettling. We also noticed that the graffiti, especially in men's restrooms, was more virulently racist than anything we had seen in the South.

After two weeks at the Holiday Inn, A.J., Marion, Jack, and I moved to the Fall Creek Parkway YMCA northwest of downtown in the historically black community in Indianapolis for a few weeks while we looked for apartments. The Y was close to Crispus Attucks High School, named for the African American soldier killed in the Boston Massacre. That school boasts a number of notable alumni, including Wes Montgomery, legendary jazz guitarist, and Oscar Robertson, who played point guard in the NBA from 1960 to 1974. In 1955, Crispus Attucks High, with Robertson as its star player, became the first all-black high school in America to win an integrated state basketball championship. They won again in 1956, becoming the first team in Indiana to have an undefeated season. We stayed a few weeks, then A.J. and I moved into White River Parkway, an apartment complex basically built for low-income residents. The rooms were small, and we did not have air-conditioning. We had planned to rent furniture while searching for accommodations that were more appropriate for my growing family. One day, early in our stay, the superintendent warned us that the complex was not safe. He was very generous and allowed us to break the lease without penalty. A.J. and I finally moved to Cloverleaf Apartments at 922c Harding Street, and I rented a large enough place to accommodate my family. Compared to our previous apartment, this seemed luxurious. It had a clubhouse, softball field, basketball court, and pool. There were two- and four-bedroom units, and each floor had a laundry room. All the appliances and utilities were included. I selected a two-bedroom unit on an upper floor, and Eddie Off, one of the older men from work, was willing to vouch for me at a local furniture store, so we were given credit for six months with no interest. This enabled me to make the apartment livable for my family. I also asked around to find a talented young pediatrician, Dr. Hudner Hobbs. She had graduated from Indiana University School of Medicine in 1965, and we were her first African American patients. She would become like a member of our family.

A.J., Marion, Jack, and I put most of our energy in that first month on learning our new jobs. Each of us had different positions at General Motors in Indianapolis. A.J. and I worked in Plant 5; I was in quality engineering, and he was in reliability. Marion and Jack both worked in Plant 3. The entire facility had about thirty thousand workers, a small percentage of which were African American. Many of these were recent hires, resulting from the company's attempts to integrate and diversify the workforce. Because we were all salaried employees, we were not part of the union, which in some ways further isolated us and made us targets for abuse. At the power plant, I don't remember seeing any racial or sexual graffiti, but it was rampant at the GM plant—on toolboxes, in lockers, and in the restrooms. We thought we had left that world behind, but there it was laid bare. Today there are laws against such behavior, but this was 1972.

I was fortunate that my supervisor, Bob Beasecker, was not resentful about having African American employees. The men in my division—Ted Hadley, Joe White, and Eddie Off—were also very professional. We came to know each other well because quality control had open work areas with ten staff members assigned to each. Our unit had two shared desks with phones on each. In my first week, I would occasionally answer the phone and hear someone yelling racial epithets. This was before caller identification, so we had no idea who it was. When the plant started hiring African American employees, there was a definite sense among the existing workers that the new quota system was taking jobs from their family members. This was made even worse when the other workers discovered that we were in salaried positions, something many hourly workers had spent years trying to secure. After a few of these calls, Joe and Eddie refused to let me answer the phone. They also took it upon themselves to protect me from that racist vitriol by making sure that I was never alone at lunch or on break. On my first day on the job, I went through the sandwich line to get a hamburger at the cafeteria and sat down at a table by myself. The next thing I knew, Ted was walking across the room to join me. I said: "You don't have to do that." But he looked me straight in the eye and said: "Yes, I do." So he invited me to come sit with some of his other white friends. The moment I sat down, one of the guys stood up in a huff and left the table. Everyone else ignored him, and I never encountered him in the lunchroom again. From that day forward, those men always made sure they had a seat for me. I am still so grateful for their kindness—because I can tell you, I was feeling pretty lonely.

Early in my tenure at GM, my boss Bob Beasecker said Robert Hicks, who oversaw engineering and quality at Detroit Diesel-Allison and was a powerful force in the industry, invited me to a meeting. So I headed to "Mahogany Row," a suite of executive offices on the top floor of Plant 5 facing the main entrance, to meet with Hicks. The name came from the lavish furniture and mahogany flooring. It was a big deal to be invited up there—and it meant you did something really good or really bad. I walked into the office not sure why I was there. Robert greeted me warmly and said, "I've noticed that you seem to know how each engine and machine works in each division. Tell me about yourself." I went on to explain my background, my time at Bethune-Cookman, and my work at the power plant. He seemed impressed and went on: "You are often here early and late. Robert says you are doing a great job, and I have been impressed with your skill and your diligence. I also hear that you all have a baby on the way." I was stunned. I had no idea that he even knew my name, and here he was talking about my family. This conversation reminded me of a talk I had with Professor Charles Cherry in college, who told me that the things that hurt or help you on a job occur when you are not in the room. Clearly, the leadership at Allison had been talking about me. That suspicion was confirmed when Robert brought up a lunch that I'd attended a few weeks earlier. I had casually mentioned that my father used to say, "You do whatever you have to do to take care of your family. No job is beneath you." I did not know that the supervisors who overheard the comment told others at the plant. My team knew me, and they wanted me to succeed.

Two important things happened as a result of the meeting and the earlier lunch. I was assigned to work on the Gas Turbine 404 (engines used in trucks and later the Patriot missile) and the T56 (used in the C130), which meant that I was regularly receiving overtime. Though a salaried employee, I had not yet moved to exempt status. My supervisor constantly found reasons for me to work on Saturday either in his area or another division, which made it possible for me to send more money home to Evelyn. Secondly, GM started investing a great deal of money and time in my training. I was sent to Flint, Michigan, to attend the General Motors Institute of Technology (GMI). Now known as Kettering University, GMI was founded as the School of Automotive Trades in 1919 and renamed Flint Institute of Technology in 1923 before being acquired by GM in 1926. It was renamed GMI six years later. Once called the "West Point of the automobile industry," the institute offered a range of classes on metals and gas turbines. I enjoyed the classes, and the instructors noticed immediately that I had much more experience than my peers and was familiar with how calipers, compressors, turbines, welding rods, and micrometers worked because of my experience at the power plant. I would go to GMI multiple times over the years for classes and seminars. In Indianapolis, I also attended classes at Indiana University–Purdue University Indianapolis (IU-PUI). Hicks also arranged and paid for one-on-one classes and became a kind of mentor to me.

One Saturday in mid-July, A.J. and I were playing basketball when I went up for a rebound and landed on another guy's foot and hurt my knee. A.J. drove me to the hospital, and after some X-rays, the doctor told me I had to stay off my leg for four weeks and could not travel. Four weeks? I did not have time to stay off it for four hours. I had only been working for six weeks, had no vacation, and was still on a probationary period with GM. So A.J. and I devised a plan. Each morning, he would come over and help me get dressed. My leg was so swollen that it took us both to force my feet into my shoes. A.J. would drive me to the front door of the plant before anyone else arrived, and I would get out and hop on one leg up the stairs. At the end of the day, we were the last to leave, and he would come and help me down the stairs. Only my closest friends at work realized I was hurt, and they kept it quiet. They became creative in contriving ways to keep me off my feet. In this way, I hid my injury from everyone else, and that was a good thing. In this era, there were not the same worker protections we have today. It was not uncommon to lose your job over such an injury. The injury also ended any chance for making extra money other than overtime at the plant. In anticipation of the birth, I regularly did odd jobs after work and on the weekends. I would rake yards, haul trash, and do basic maintenance for the landlord. But that revenue stream ended because I could hardly stand.

From June to October, I did not see a single member of my family. It was too expensive for me to return to Fort Pierce and the injury added additional complications, so I had to depend on our families to help support Evelyn. My mother was especially doting, and they became very close. Evelyn had an uneventful pregnancy, and in her sixth month, we found out that we were having twins. It is difficult to be pregnant in the South in the summer, but Evelyn managed to stay inside during the hottest part of the day and take long walks early in the morning or late in the evening. She was due in October, so we spent most of our time on the phone to stay connected. On Friday, August 7, while we were talking, Evelyn told me that she thought the babies were coming early. The comment went over my head, but later that night I received a call that her water broke while she was taking a bath to relax. She called my mother to tell her that she was on her way, and my mother was so excited that she beat Evelyn and her mother to the hospital.

On Tuesday, August 8, my twin sons were born. Roderick came first at 12:32 and Broderick at 12:37 p.m. I was told later that you could hear my mother enthusiastically telling everyone who came within earshot that she had two new grandbabies. Evelyn and I were both worried because the boys weighed a little more than three pounds each and had to remain in the neonatal intensive care unit. Broderick was allowed to come home in three weeks, but Roderick had to stay in the neonatal intensive care unit for nearly a month. Because I was injured and still on my six-month probationary period, I was unable to travel home to see the boys. I was devastated but knew that I did not have anything to worry about because our families made sure Evelyn and the boys had everything they needed.

I remember a few days after the birth, I was at the coffee machine and saw Mr. Hicks. He had come to congratulate me and asked me when I was going to get to meet the boys. I replied: "I'm going to stay here to work on this project and make sure I meet all of my obligations. I did not want to violate the probationary period and am trying to be as conscientious as possible. My extended family is helping

Evelyn." He was a little surprised and finally said: "You can't imagine how impressed I am with that answer." I knew how important my job was going to be to the future of my family. He saw that it was one of my guiding principles, and I did not want to do anything to jeopardize that. It turned out to be the right decision. I was reminded of what my father used to say, "You have to put your family's security above everything." A short-time sacrifice was worth a long-term advantage.

While thrilled the boys were here, we were worried about the expense that we were now facing. My mother worked at the hospital. Without telling us, she was prepared to have fifty dollars taken out of her weekly paycheck to pay for the prenatal care. Luckily, we did not need the funds because my insurance from GM took over. Not many children in the hospital at Fort Pierce had insurance from one of the top companies in the nation. In mid-September, when the boys were viable enough to travel, Evelyn's brother Melvin drove the three of them to Indianapolis. Evelyn remembers it as a harrowing trip—1,079 miles with two premature infants without air-conditioning. Our parents were nervous wrecks during the journey and did not relax until Evelyn and the boys arrived. I was so relieved and grateful to see Evelyn get out of the car with the babies, and I remember how I felt while holding and hugging them. They smiled at me like they knew who I was. We were blessed to have neighbors Chris and Ralph Tolan help us in those early days. They took us shopping, babysat the twins, and cooked us dinner. She was German, and he was from Indiana, and they had two children, Judy and Susan. They became dear friends. Roderick and Broderick were happy babies; if one woke up, he would play with his toes or fingers until the other one was awake. They loved to keep each other company.

In the summer of 1973, we made a big decision that Evelyn would return to Florida A&M in August to finish her student teaching so she could complete her undergraduate degree in education. The whole family was supportive of the decision, especially Evelyn's father. He had taught her to care for herself, to be independent, and never to depend on someone else for money. Our parents helped us develop a plan to care for the twins, who had just celebrated their first birthday. Evelyn's parents, Louise and Jonathan, whom we fondly called Buster, would be the primary caregivers for the boys, with help from my parents and our extended family. Evelyn moved into a dorm on campus that fall semester and taught at Florida A&M Elementary School. On the weekends, she made the six-hour drive from Tallahassee to Fort Pierce to see the boys, returning to school on Sunday.

While Evelyn and the boys were gone, I worked long hours at the plant. I ate most of my meals there, cooked a bit at home, and was hosted by the Tolans occasionally for dinner. That hard work paid off, and in November 1973, I was in for a surprise. Chuck Alsacker, the superintendent of the shop floor, was an avowed racist, and he made no secret of his disdain for GM's recent minority hires. He was not somebody to trust. But that fall, I received a call that he wanted to make me his first African American supervisor, at the age of twenty-three. I was stunned; this man was someone to fear.

When Chuck offered me the job, I had to ask why he selected me. He replied, "I pass you all the time on my way to meetings upstairs, and you are always working. I asked around and found out that you are productive and never seem to be wasting time. You dress well; you do not complain; and you are a family man. I have objected from the beginning to bringing colored folks to the shop floor as supervisors. But if I was going to bring one, I wanted to choose the right person, not just because he was black. I do not feel I am cheating anybody by putting you out here. If I am going to take a bet on somebody, I'm going to bet on you." Supervisors for bargaining unit employees made at least 25 percent more than their top five employees. So this meant that I was about to receive a 40 percent increase in my salary, plus a cost-of-living increase. Now if you are black in America, you have a keen sense that whites are watching you all the time. I remember writer James Baldwin talking about "a little white man deep inside of all of us"—criticizing and waiting for us to screw up. In this case, Alsacker was watching me, but for the right reasons.

He saw me demonstrate behaviors that told him I could be a leader, that he wanted others to emulate. He knew me, and he provided me with an extraordinary opportunity—a priceless gift. He helped me see that building your brand was an important lesson, one that I would pass on when I found myself in a position of power.

CHAPTER 5
AND WE RISE

"I was young, black, and an inexperienced manager— not a great place to be."

WHILE GENERAL MOTORS is often seen as an automotive company located in Detroit, it developed various automotive-component and nonautomotive brands, many headquartered outside of Michigan. Subsidiaries included Euclid and Terex (construction equipment and vehicles in Ohio); Electro-Motive Diesel (locomotive, marine, and industrial diesel engines in Ohio and Illinois); Frigidaire (appliances in Indiana); New Departure (bearings in Connecticut); Delco Electronics and ACDelco (electrical and electronic components in Indiana); GM Defense (military vehicles in Michigan); and Electronic Data Systems (information technology in Texas). Two of those companies, Detroit Diesel (automotive and industrial diesel engines) and Allison (aircraft engines, transmissions, and gas turbine engines), merged on September 1, 1970, to create Detroit Diesel-Allison, a company that would dramatically shape and define my career for eighteen years.

This was an exciting period of consolidation and growth. The merger of the two companies brought together more than eighty years of combined experience and helped launch a range of new products that included: gas turbine engines (GT404, GT740), a new automatic electric shaft control that offered power shift transmission to heavy construction equipment, the 250-C20B and 250-B17B (turboshaft for helicopters and turboprop for fixed-wing aircraft), the v-730 (a fully automatic v-730 transmission), and the Model 570 (a 7,000 horsepower gas turbine engine for industrial power generation and marine work). In 1973 the company opened a new training headquarters in Indianapolis and the next year started construction on the 664,000 square foot addition to Plant 12. In March 1975, three years after I started at the plant, we were awarded a four-year $11.3 million contract by the U.S. Army to design and develop an 800 horsepower class turboshaft engine known as the GMA500. A year later, the XM1 tank was unveiled.

The year after my graduation from Bethune-Cookman was a whirlwind. In June 1972, I moved from Fort Pierce, Florida, to Indianapolis, Indiana, to start my new job at Detroit Diesel-Allison, a GM subsidiary. Evelyn gave birth to our twin boys in August, and they joined me in Indianapolis in September. A year later, in October 1973, at the age of twenty-three, I began my new role as the day shift supervisor for manufacturing inspection. I had been working at Plant 5 for a little more than a year in quality engineering before being tapped for my first leadership role. This was a big change—I moved from sitting upstairs at a desk writing quality control manuals to being on the shop floor inspecting the 149 Diesel and Electric Motor that was used in aircraft, trains, and automobiles. My shift, from 6:30 a.m. to 3:00 p.m., involved overseeing a team of thirteen unionized hourly workers to verify the quality of the parts made by manufacturing at the plant. Our team did a variety of special testing, and the shop floor was filled with machines and tools as well as tables filled with blueprints. Our unit focused on quality, performance, and safety—we had to look at each component that went into the engines. If something was defective or inoperable, we had to go back to the manufacturing department to see how it might be improved. In the early 1970s, there was not a lot of automation, so all of this work was done by hand.

I was overseeing just one unit in manufacturing inspection; there were about forty to forty-five other units doing similar work in the plant. I was the youngest person in my area and one of two or three African Americans in a supervisory role in the inspection area. They were all like me—young, recent college graduates. My team included manufacturing inspectors or process layout inspectors. Only one member of my team, Jerry Crane, had a college degree, from Purdue, and he was brilliant and very professional. The rest were all highly skilled in various technical fields. They had trade degrees and had completed on-the-job training or apprenticeships. Most of the employees I supervised were old enough to be my parents. So here I am, a black man who looked like a teenager, as their new boss. Most of the white employees had never been in close proximity to black people—they went to different schools, stores, barbershops, and churches and lived in largely segregated neighborhoods. Few had experience working with blacks and almost none had been supervised by one. I was young, black, and an inexperienced manager—not a great place to be. My only redeeming quality was that I really knew the equipment. My work at the power plant, my training at the General Motors Institute in Flint in my first year, and my knowledge of plant operations gave me some credibility with a team that had every reason to reject me. I also tried to remember my mother's adage, "Humble is always better than arrogant."

I knew that in order to do well in this new position, I had to be deliberate in building my brand. I was guided by the question my mother used to ask me ("How will they know you?") and focused on bolstering my reputation and strategic alliances in those early days. I knew I had one chance to make a good first impression, so I mapped out a strategy. I continued the practice of showing up early, staying late, and returning from lunch and coffee breaks early. I tried to be well informed about who was on my team and sought to be both fair and constructive with both praise and criticism. I walked the shop floor constantly, talking to people to find out what they did, what they needed, and helped when I could. It was clear from the outset that there was a lot of mistrust between salaried and union employees, and I tried not to exacerbate the situation. I thought the best approach to my new position was to be consistent and predictable. I never openly criticized the union or their negotiations and kept my interactions as professional as possible. I tried to remind the team that our job was to inspect the parts so we could serve the customer at the highest level. If something was wrong, it was our job to fix it without shaming our colleagues in manufacturing or other units. I always made two of my priorities clear—safety and clean facilities.

Though committed to my plan, it was still difficult to overcome the constant sense of conflict and sense that each side was trying to undermine the other. One afternoon, I was on the shop floor talking with Bob Zimmerman, who worked in my unit and was from Martinsville. Our conversation must have looked pretty animated, because all of a sudden the general supervisor appeared. Assuming we were arguing, he forced himself in our conversation with the goal of defending me, a fellow member of the management team. Bob and I both started laughing because we had been talking about motocross racing. We were joking about motorcycles, and I was teasing him in a good-hearted way about a recent incident when he was thrown from his bike. When the general supervisor realized the content of our conversation, he became frustrated, told us to get back to work, and stormed off. This small interaction revealed how powerful the distrust was between management and the union workers.

To complicate matters, both the union committeeman (Tom Ford) and the alternate committeeman (John Finch) were assigned to my unit. Tom was brilliant, and John, for some reason, always believed my father was a lawyer, and so he treated me with a great deal of respect. I found out later that Cleo Miller, who worked with John, started that rumor to help boost my credibility. As the main union representatives, they were not supposed to like me. Their job was to serve as liaisons between labor and management and represent employee interests in the event of a problem or complaint. They also served as the union's on-floor representatives to ensure that management lived up to their contractual obligations. Their jobs were adversarial by their very nature, so I thought my best course of action was to understand the issues that they raised and find a way to speak candidly without making them look bad in front of their members. It took several months for us to trust each other, but the hard work paid off. I recall one incident that was particularly instructive.

Tom was very good at his job, and in this era, the management often required the committeeman to work the first hour of his shift before he could attend to union business. This was often a ploy to remind the union that management was really in charge, and it grated on Tom's nerves. This power play caused me more grief than anything else in my entire day, and it was a constant aggravation. Tom complained, the union members were mad, and management made a point of making him an example. One day after work, I was pumping gas at a nearby service station and saw Tom at the next pump. We greeted each other, and I started laughing when I told him, "Tom, you cause me more grief than anyone, but I know it's not your fault." We could never have had a conversation like this at the plant—it was just too political. I had learned that you have to create a safe space to communicate honestly; in this case it was the gas station. We talked for a while and came up with a plan that would put an end to the problem once and for all. Every day, he would spend that first hour writing scrap tickets (these were inspection tickets that accounted for anything that was unusable so it could be removed from the plant inventory). In the afternoons before the end of the shift, members of my team would collect scrap to make sure Tom had something to do each morning. If they could not find anything, he would just inventory the same pieces repeatedly and not submit the paperwork. This plan solved our problem and both sides felt they had won. Tom saved face with his union colleagues, and the management left Tom alone because they felt he was accommodating them.

While a silly exercise, we both understood that it was an important way for everyone to win. I came to understand that each person had to play to his or her constituency. Tom would never have been elected if he were perceived as someone who kowtowed to management, and management would not look good if they gave in too easily to the union. This plan helped them both save face and helped me understand what was motivating both sides. My treatment of Tom also sent signals to the union and my fellow managers that there was another way to get the job done. Conflict was not inevitable; we could work together. But the culture was really hard to change, and

I saw a lot of screaming, cursing, and other misbehavior in the plant. To some degree, this was generational. The new, younger hires who had not worked in manufacturing for decades had no memories of intractable union-management conflict. Because of this, they were often willing to be more collaborative.

I recall another incident that illustrated the power of regional stereotypes. Cleo Miller worked in manufacturing and was responsible for sanding off ragged edges, cleaning out passages, and cleaning parts after they had been produced. We were both at the plant early one morning, and he asked me if I wanted some biscuits and gravy. Knowing I was from the South, he thought he would share a taste of home with me. The problem was that midwestern biscuits and gravy are not the same thing as southern biscuits and gravy, and I had not acquired a taste for the midwestern version. But I also knew that this was not going to end well if I did not accept his kind offer. So to avoid hurting his feelings, I took a bite, but I nearly gagged. Cleo, who was also African American, started laughing and said: "What kind of brother are you?" For the rest of the time we worked together, he called me "Gravy."

My unit inspected four production areas in the plant: (1) blocks for diesel engines; (2) rods, bearings, and adaptors for diesel engines; (3) flywheels, covers, and pump housings; and (4) turbines for electromotive engines. Wilson Burns, who was white, was the general supervisor over these four units that I inspected, and Ernest Vaughn, who was black, supervised production of the flywheels, covers, and pump housing. Manufacturing and inspection were often at odds with each other because if something goes wrong there is a tendency to blame the other side. I recall one incident when a bunch of cylinders came off the block line that were cut incorrectly and were unusable. This was a big deal; supervisors were regularly fired for such mistakes because they were costly and undermined efficiency. After some finger pointing, we were all called into a meeting to determine how to resolve the issue. About ten minutes into the meeting, Wilson spoke up, "My people cut the cylinders wrong, and Lee's team doesn't have any responsibility in this matter. We have to fix it on our end."

My respect for him increased exponentially that day, and an incident on the football field helped transform that respect into friendship. When my twin boys were about four, I took them to Northwest High School to watch a junior football league play their games. My sons, Roderick and Broderick, were intensely interested in what the older boys were doing and quickly learned that the object of the game was to catch the ball and run with it. Between one of the quarters, the official placed the ball on the field as the teams walked off to meet with their coaches. Unbeknownst to me, Roderick and Broderick ran onto the field and grabbed the ball. All of a sudden I see a scramble of referees and parents chasing the boys down the field. Out of the corner of my eye, I saw Wilson Burns, one of the league coaches, laughing at the whole scene. That was the beginning of our families' friendship, and he became a mentor to me, friend to Evelyn, and uncle to the boys. Wilson later became head of operations and procurement and a plant manager. He would eventually become my boss and regularly sent me to classes focused on leadership. We remained close until his death in 2019.

I had a less auspicious start with Ernest Vaughn, who supervised the production of the flywheels, covers, and pump housings that my team inspected. In our first few months working together, I thought he was mean and inconsiderate, but I soon learned that first impressions are sometimes wrong. We both later discovered that our teams had put us in adversarial positions. One Saturday, we both found ourselves at the plant. Ernie was ten years my senior and a veteran, and he approached me to talk about how to improve our relationship. It was a good conversation, and we addressed the resentments that had been festering. Like Wilson, Ernie would become a great friend and our ticket to the social life in Indianapolis. He and another coworker, Tim Higgins, both grew up in the city and helped us integrate into our new home and community. Tim introduced me to Mack's Barber Shop on Thirtieth Street, and to this day Broderick, who is a doctor in Indianapolis, still has his hair cut there. They helped our family find Crooked Creek Baptist Church on 5540 North Michigan Road, where we remained until I moved to Atlanta. Broderick is still a member, and I remember that the pastor, Orville Sutton, sold me my first set of golf clubs. I owe all of that to Ernie.

In 1974, I moved from day shift supervisor to the afternoon shift, doing manufacturing inspection for the same four areas and for Redford gears. I received a 5 percent raise, and my hours changed dramatically, and I arrived at work at 2:15 to start the shift at 3:00 p.m. and finished at 11:30, arriving home around midnight. This had a dramatic impact on my family, and Evelyn had to become both mother and father to the boys. I saw them early in the morning and on weekends, but the rest of the time, Evelyn was in charge. We did not know then that it would be a dress rehearsal for an illness that would nearly cripple me two years later.

I liked the new position, and my team grew from thirteen to seventeen employees. I quickly discovered that the afternoon shift gave me more opportunities, especially when a fellow supervisor went on vacation. I was often asked to supervise their area and became familiar with the operations of a large number of units. The experience was invaluable, and I always assumed that this cross-training was orchestrated by Wilson Burns and Dan Duncan. In these years, I gained experience overseeing production teams, which was a new area for me. I also found the afternoon shift to be more socially active and relaxed than the day shift. I joined bowling, basketball, and softball leagues and was occasionally invited to play golf on the weekend, though I was not very good and did not like taking the time away from my family. Because the top-level supervisors worked the day shift, the afternoon shift was less bureaucratic and tense. The distrust that was so palpable between management and the union workers during the day was noticeably absent on this later shift. Supervisors and union leaders communicated more freely in the afternoons, which created a more productive working environment.

Broderick and Roderick continued to grow and thrive and became very protective of each other. Like most twins, they had their own language and only communicated to adults when they needed something. They attended preschool at Westside Christian Schools (sponsored by Westside Church of the Nazarene) that had been recommended by a friend and was close to our house. Being new to the area, we were not fully aware of the problems related to the Indianapolis school district—efforts to desegregate in the 1960s and 1970s led to busing and the creation of separate white private schools. We sent the boys to Westside, a private preschool, so remained largely oblivious to the conditions on the ground. We found out, fairly quickly, that most African American children went to public school, so Roderick and Broderick were often the only black students in their classes. In their first few months at preschool, Roderick refused to take a nap, exercising his role as big brother. He would lay down and watch Broderick sleep to make sure he was safe. We could never understand why Roderick was so tired when he got home each day. We finally spoke to his preschool teacher, Miss Pam, who told us what was happening. Overall, though, they loved school, and we were pleased that the school was so protective of the boys.

Evelyn's decision to return to teaching when the boys were about to start kindergarten exposed us to a much darker side of race and public education in Indianapolis. We lived near Wayne Township Schools, so Evelyn worked as a substitute teacher at William Penn School 49 (at 1720 West Wilkins Street). On her first day, the city experienced one of the worst ice storms in the city. Ice was everywhere, but she somehow made it to and from school. She enjoyed the work and became friendly with the teachers and principal. But we started to notice an odd pattern—the school only called her to substitute on inclement weather days. Tired of the sporadic nature of the job, she decided to put in an application for a full-time position. Even though there were a number of teaching positions advertised, the principal told her that they were not hiring. She became suspicious when she heard our neighbor, Chris, talking about visiting the elementary school to drop off her daughters and seeing so many new teachers. So Evelyn started to do a little research and found an article in the local newspaper featuring all of the new faculty members that had been hired in the township for the next school year. The next day, Evelyn made an appointment with the superintendent and asked about the positions, not betraying that she had a copy of that article in her purse. He was clearly uncomfortable with the conversation and started making excuses. It became clear that something was terribly wrong.

Later that evening, she told me what happened, and several of my colleagues at work told me to contact the Indianapolis district office of the Equal Employment Opportunity Commission (EEOC). Title VII of the Civil Rights Act of 1964 created the EEOC, and local offices were established around the country. We did not want to sue the school district; we just wanted to make sure that everyone had a fair shot. After completing the necessary paperwork, we did not think much more about it as Evelyn continued her job search. Two months later, we received a call from Shirley Swaniger that the EEOC completed a formal investigation and that the district wanted to settle our case. We did not really understand the process and did not even know that an investigation had happened, but we were pleased to see that it had been taken seriously. The school district ultimately paid Evelyn a settlement, and she found a job in the Indianapolis Public School District at William McKinley School 39 teaching fourth grade. The school was farther from our house than the ones in Wayne Township, but she felt fortunate to be employed because the nation was in the midst of a recession. The U.S. Bureau of Labor Statistics estimated that 2.3 million jobs were lost between 1973 and 1975; at the time, this was a postwar record. By May 1975, unemployment reached 9 percent, and the effects of the recession were felt into the middle of Ronald Reagan's first term as president.

There is an ironic twist to Evelyn's story. Because of the turmoil over desegregation and the advent of busing in the 1970s, Indianapolis lost hundreds of teachers. Eventually a judge forced the suburban townships to hire African American teachers from the city schools, and that is how Evelyn ended up teaching at Chapel Glen Elementary, Rhodes Elementary, and North Wayne Elementary, three schools in Wayne Township. The district that rejected her was where she would spend twenty-five years of her career.

During this period, we returned home to Florida to visit family twice a year, especially when the boys were young. I remember that a year or two after we married, my mother pulled me aside one evening and urged me to encourage Evelyn to visit her family often because they were very close, and keeping her from them would damage our relationship. I heeded her advice, and during the summers, I would visit for a week and return to work. Evelyn and the boys would stay a bit longer because she was off in the summers. For the first four or five years, we would return home to celebrate Christmas in Florida, but that became increasingly difficult as my job responsibilities continued to grow.

The visits were not always relaxing, and I remember that one of my coworkers at the plant, Wilson Burns, and I were talking about visiting our families. I do not recall what prompted the conversation, but I do remember that he said, "Lee Ernest, I want to tell you something so you are not disappointed. You will find that when you go back home, not everybody is happy about your success. You will find that people are petty and jealous." Years later, I found myself in an audience listening to Dr. Crawford Loritts, senior pastor of Fellowship Bible Church in Roswell, Georgia, and he explained that some people think that your success means that something has been stolen from them, and they will constantly find reasons to discredit you. This was true for me, but only part of the story. Our relationship with our family and friends changed when we moved to Indianapolis because we were so far away, our social and financial situation had changed, and we found that a few members of our family begrudged our success. We had left our small town in Florida to move to an urban, bustling midwestern city, and maintained strong connections to those who were closest to us.

In 1975, I moved again to become the dayshift manager inspecting T56 and 502 vanes, gearboxes, housings, and covers. While I had an easy transition into my first two supervisory positions, I soon learned that not everyone was supportive of this promotion. Kenny Doss was the night supervisor who took over when I finished at 3:00 p.m., and I later learned that the superintendent, Elmer Brown, asked him to report back anytime I made a mistake. Elmer made his dislike for me obvious, and Kenny served as a spy. But the more Kenny and I worked together, the more we talked, and after about six months he confessed: "Lee, when you were transferred over here, I started out hating you, then that moved to dislike. But I've discovered that you're really good at your job. You are always trying and really give GM their money's worth." I think that was his way of showing me respect, and we became good partners. In fact, years later, I hired Kenny and promoted him to superintendent. He became a beloved friend, and I still miss him dearly.

Because I was now in a different unit, I no longer had the support of Chuck Alsacker, the superintendent of the shop floor, who had first promoted me. While I had witnessed covert racism at the plant before, it was now overt. Elmer made it clear that he did not support GM's efforts to diversify the workforce and that he had been forced to hire me. The general supervisor who worked under Elmer, Paul Nicholas, was unsupportive and unpleasant. And I was not their only target. Many of the hourly, unionized workers hated working in such a hostile environment. In some ways, the vitriol that I endured bound us together. In this position, I learned an important lesson—the success of an organization depends as much on the subordinates as it does on the top leadership. A toxic superintendent or supervisor can make or break a unit. But the hourly workers were equally important, and as much as Elmer and Paul wanted me to fail, the hourly workers I supervised wanted me to succeed. Paul and I mended our relationship, and I later was instrumental in hiring his son.

In the fall of 1976, I had a terrifying health scare, and my work situation made this even more stressful. I was diagnosed with a rare disorder in which my body's immune system started attacking my nerves. It started with weakness and tingling and threatened to paralyze my entire body. Each day, I found myself weaker, until I could no longer stand. It was terrifying. I met with a surgeon who said he was unable to find a pulse in my leg and told me that I required a complicated operation on my veins and that I might never walk again. I was only twenty-six years old. Hoping for better news from a second opinion, I met with Dr. Robert McCallum, my general practitioner, who correctly diagnosed me and was skeptical of the surgeon's strategy. He called the surgeon, and they ended up in a heated debate. McCallum came to the same conclusion that I did— that the surgeon only wanted to do the procedure for the money and was unwilling to even consider less invasive options that were more conventional treatments for my condition. I learned that I needed intravenous immunoglobulins but faced a recovery that could last from a few weeks to a few years. I was so grateful for Dr. McCallum's intervention. He sent me to an orthopedist, who helped develop a rehabilitation plan that offered supportive care and physical therapy. He was more than a doctor; he was my friend.

This experience exposed how tenuous my job was—here I was a young African American man with a major handicap. This was fourteen years before the Americans with Disabilities Act (ADA) became law. There were not many protections for injured employees. The plant did not have ramps or accessible bathrooms. It would have been easy for GM to simply have given up on me and found a replacement. It would have been easy for any of my supervisors to try to terminate me. I learned a very important lesson during this illness—no matter how hard I worked, no matter how much I built my brand, I was, in the end, expendable.

CHAPTER 6
MAHOGANY ROW

"I would not learn much if they refused to tell me what I was doing wrong or were reluctant to call me out for being a young punk."

I N 1976, I FOUND MYSELF DISABLED. I was twenty-six years old and had been at Detroit Diesel-Allison, a subsidiary of General Motors, for four years. Roderick, the older of my twin sons, who was just four years old, said to me one morning that he could not love me if I could not walk, and it hit me like a ton of bricks. I had long believed that if you got a good education, worked hard, were both honest and loyal, and did your job well, you were safe. That belief came crashing down that fall, and I learned a powerful lesson that I have never forgotten.

To help in my recovery from an immune system condition, I was first given braces and then crutches. Learning to walk as an adult is an extremely difficult enterprise—much harder than most people think. It is as if your body has lost all muscle memory, and recreating even most basic movements is almost impossible. It took me about a month before I could take a few steps without assistance, and I had to take a leave of absence from my job. I later learned that one of the superintendents was trying to get me fired. When I came back full time in January 1977, I was still really struggling. My shift started at 3:00 p.m., so I arrived at 1:45, and it took me nearly an hour and fifteen minutes in those early weeks to walk through the department.

Before the accident, I could cover the same ground in less than fifteen minutes. I never talked much about the injury, but everybody knew that I was suffering. The hourly workers rallied around me because they knew that people were harassing me. Ever resourceful, they found an electric scooter to help ferry me around the plant. I never had to ask for help; they just paid attention, and the scooter would magically appear when I needed to move around the shop floor. Even with that assistance, I had to walk a lot—about three to five miles a day. I recall being so tired at the end of my shift that I had to give myself a pep talk to walk to my car to drive home. This was a period of labor unrest, when management and labor were often at odds. Ironically, the hourly workers were my staunchest allies during this period. They felt obligated to protect one of their own; I was their supervisor, and they were determined to help me and our unit succeed.

This entire ordeal exposed me to my vulnerabilities, made me rethink just how fragile my life was. This was a very dark time, and I wallowed in self-doubt and self-pity. Here I was twenty-six years old, with a great job, beautiful wife, two precocious twin boys, and I could not get out of bed. I give Evelyn and the boys a lot of credit. They offered me an endless stream of encouragement, but it was still hard. Evelyn brought a quiet strength to my recovery. She had grown up in the South working in tomato fields in a poor family, so I knew she was tough. But she was also so kind and polite that I often underestimated her strength. She took over running the household and leading our family without making me feel useless. Evelyn continued with her job, managing the boys' hectic schedules, caring for the house, and making sure we stayed engaged in the community. Each night, I heard her putting the twins to bed and praying for my recovery. Because I was suffering, I became so focused on my pain that I could not see what was right in front of me—my struggle and illness was taking a heavy toll on my wife and children. I was humbled, and now I understand why people turn to drugs and alcohol to help survive situations like this. The therapy and Dr. McCallum's persistence in helping me recover paid off. I started walking but had to wear the braces for months and the orthopedic shoes for the next fifteen years. Nobody could tell because I could hide them with long pants.

This ordeal—the illness and my long road to recovery—helped me come to grips with the fact that I was—like every worker in America—expendable. What felt like a curse actually turned out to be a blessing in the long trajectory of my career. Recognizing that I was replaceable gave me a more realistic perspective on job security and the importance of remaining relevant. In the 1970s and 1980s, it was still possible to take a job with a single company and remain there for your entire career. Today, that is almost unheard of. The Bureau of Labor Statistics reported in 2018 that the median employee tenure for men was 4.3 years, and for women 4.0 years. In the era in which I was at General Motors, it was fairly common to work with people who had been there for three or four decades. My illness motivated me to retool constantly, to seek additional opportunities to further my education and cross-train in other units, and to avoid complacency. What I experienced at a young age—feeling useless— still helps me today when I counsel retiring executives who struggle to find their value as they step away from their careers.

About eighteen months after the vaccine incident, in 1978, I was promoted to general supervisor on the afternoon shift, overseeing ten supervisors and about five hundred unionized employees. Facing my vulnerabilities empowered me, and I seized the opportunity to rethink what I could do and what I might become. This motivated me to approach this position in a very deliberate way, focusing on mastering leadership principles that would help shape the rest of my career. Before my illness, I had been steadily progressing in my career, reacting to situations that arose, and accepting what was put in front of me. After the illness, I started to imagine what might be possible for me and my family. I immediately recognized that I needed to polish my leadership skills and brand myself as a key decision maker to continue to remain relevant.

In my first four years at General Motors, I was fortunate to find colleagues and mentors at the plant that helped me navigate the racial and political climate fairly effectively. Now I was going to actively seek out elder statesmen who were respected, effective, and generous with their time. I realized that the key to my success was going to be to observe and engage with these men, to try to glean as much insight about the company and about management as I could in the shortest amount of time. My quest was guided by a host of questions: Why were their units so productive? How did they respond to mistakes and errors? What strategies did they use to motivate their unionized employees? How did they mitigate conflict? What qualities did they exhibit that I could emulate? I needed their guidance and wisdom but did not have the luxury of investing two decades to get it. But I also needed their honesty. I would not learn much if they refused to tell me what I was doing wrong or were reluctant to call me out for being a young punk. Simultaneously, I had to overcome my own ego and not get frustrated and walk away when they criticized me. It was hard to have somebody blister your sense of self and then come back for more. But I did, and Billy Wright, Tim Ross, Dan Duncan, Pat Laughlin, Cleo Miller, Willie Bonner, Dennis Sumpter, Kenny Doss, Ernie Vaughn, Bob Brown, Wilson Burns, and Jim Lunsford stayed with me. Billy especially stood out during this period; he was the one who pulled the shirtless stunt in my office that I talk about in the introduction. He had an innate ability to give constructive advice and was never threatened by anyone else's success.

Looking back, I did not realize how fortunate I was to have had Don Goode as my superintendent for a time. He made a point of showing me how the business worked from a financial perspective. He used to tell me, "Act like you belong, and make them prove that you don't." During breaks and before and after work, he would sit with me and review spreadsheets and account statements to help me understand the money side of the business. To further expand my skills, the company sent me to a financial management course, and it was obvious that I was one of the youngest people in the class and one of the only African Americans. I found myself with an intense bout of imposter syndrome. What was I doing here, and what could I possibly contribute? At the first class, I spent most of my time looking around the room at the seasoned professionals who had a lot more experience than I did. I still do not know who funded my participation, but it was expensive and intense. The three-week course met every day, and I felt as if I had completed an MBA in finance when I was finished. During this same period, I was offered temporary assignments in other units and divisions, in some cases for up to six months at a time. I never knew who arranged them, but it was clear that they were grooming me for more responsibility.

The 1970s were an exciting time but also an anxious time to work in manufacturing. Apart from occasional labor disputes, there was a sense that the world was shifting beneath our feet. There were so many changes—social, generational, economic, racial, and political—that dominated the headlines. Additional changes in labor relations, global markets, foreign competition, technology, the military, and warfare created a recipe for uncertainty. In the early 1970s, the United States was hit with a major gas crisis that would reshape the auto industry for decades. The era of big American cars and cheap fuel was over, and this would negatively impact GM, of which Detroit Diesel-Allison was a subsidiary. By the 1980s, German and Japanese car imports became popular, and GM was struggling under its obligations to retirees. There was also an erosion of authority. Younger workers did not share the same expectations and loyalties as older workers, nor did they have the same unquestioning respect for the chain of command. They were more comfortable with a diversified workforce, were less willing to follow orders blindly, and embraced new technologies that often made more seasoned workers uncomfortable. I found myself in an unusual situation—I was young enough to be inspired by the change but also seasoned enough to understand its complexity and long-term impact on the industry.

As I regained my strength and embraced my new position, my family continued to thrive. The twins remained at Westside Christian Schools until fourth grade. They were good students and talented athletes and especially enjoyed playing basketball. Because they were popular and two of a handful of African American students in a private school, they were largely insulated from the tense racial climate that dominated the public schools in this era of integration. But we soon learned that they were not entirely immune from its ill effects. One Friday night, the Westside team played a team from Mooresville Christian Academy. Broderick and Roderick were on the basketball court playing in the last few minutes of the game. Westside Christian was about to win when one of the parents from the other school started shouting racial epithets from the bleachers. The twins were the only black children on the court, so it was clear that the slurs were directed at them. Our coach, Buddy Zacharis, who was white, jumped up from his courtside seat and ran toward the offending Mooresville parent. Evelyn and I did not understand what was happening because we did not hear it, but suddenly chaos erupted. Several fathers from our team rushed onto the court to restrain Buddy. Some of the Westside families started shouting at the Mooresville parent and forced him out of the gym. Just like with the unionized employees who helped me get the scooter when I was injured, the Westside community rallied around us. In this instance, we were not just a black family in Indianapolis in the 1970s. We were a Westside family that had been wronged, and nobody was going to let that stand without a response. This was supposed to be a Christian league, and the parent had clearly crossed the line. While the boys rarely faced incidents this blatant, it was clear that racism in Indianapolis was festering just below the surface. We never knew when it would bubble up—when Evelyn applied for a job or when the boys were about to win a basketball game—but it was always there.

My hard work as general supervisor paid off, and in 1981, I was promoted to plant superintendent. My experience in management, background in finance, and the relationships I cultivated doing temporary assignments in different units throughout the plant made me a logical candidate for the position. I also enjoyed a positive relationship with the union that was built on a deep sense of mutual respect. In some ways, the plant came to seem like Virgil's machine shop at the power plant where I worked at a teenager. People worked together, were willing to troubleshoot, and did not fear innovation and change. I had reached Level 8 in the plant, which gave me more responsibility for budgets and operations, and because of the strong training and informal apprenticeships I had enjoyed, I was ready. I also came to understand from the informal group of mentors that I had assembled that success was not always a popularity contest, but it was essential not to have people actively working against you. There were plenty of people who disliked me for one reason or another, but the vast majority were not trying to sabotage my work. In a large plant with complex operations, the best you could hope for was neutrality. You cannot survive in this environment without it.

In this position, I was sent on my first overseas trips to purchase machinery and visit other plants. In 1982, I traveled to Tokyo, where we sent kits for the T-56 engine, and we visited the plants to provide some quality control for the Japanese workers. They had a very different work culture, one truly focused on collaboration and cooperation, not competition. As a result, their workers bonded into strong teams and were quick to identify and solve problems. This helped explain their coming dominance of the auto industry and manufacturing more generally. During the two-month visit, we learned a great deal about efficiency. Several years later, I traveled to England, Germany, and Switzerland to look at different types of equipment for gear manufacturing and heat treat (industrial, thermal, and metalworking processes). It was illuminating to see how the machinery was constructed and equally important to get a close look at our competition. The trips really helped broaden my sense of the global marketplace as it related to manufacturing.

It might seem like my path at Detroit Diesel-Allison was just a constant climb up the ladder to success, but this was not the case. I received regular promotions but often competed against colleagues who were brighter and more skilled than I was. But I had one advantage. I had learned important lessons during my illness—never settle into a routine that will lead to complacency, always keep reading and learning, respect the people you manage, and try to anticipate issues before they become problems. In large companies where people spend their whole careers, it was easy to become entrenched, inflexible, and fearful of change. That was something I tried to avoid, but I still made plenty of mistakes. The biggest one was not surrounding myself with good people once I became the superintendent. When I moved into this position, a number of my informal mentors told me that I did not have a good team. I inherited some problems, but others I hired myself. Dan Duncan, Wilson Burns, and Bob Brown, a retired army lieutenant colonel who had a previous career as a fighter pilot, were especially helpful to me during this period. I met Bob when I worked in my first position in quality control, and he later became a plant manager. He, along with Wilson, had been watching me. In any other plant, we would have been competitors, but Bob and Wilson saw me struggling and stepped in to help. Wilson had a generous spirit and would sit in my office after my shift and review production sheets, budgets, anything that would give him a full sense of what was going wrong. He finally told me, "Your people are not being honest with you; they are transferring data, putting in incomplete numbers, and not reporting accurately." Here I was—with nearly ten years at the plant—leading an underperforming team. Another manager, Dan Duncan, whom I had worked with for years, showed up one day and said, "I am going to transfer some of my employees from the night shift to the afternoon shift to help you." Bob, Wilson, and Dan taught me that hiring and cultivating talent was not an occasional activity addressed only when we had a vacancy but part of the strategic work that contributed to success. I started focusing on building effective teams by concentrating less on emotion and more on expertise, competency, and fit. I also refined my management style, investing my team with authority, being transparent with my decision making, clearly articulating the job duties and my expectations during the hiring process, and offering frequent, constructive feedback to new employees.

Detroit Diesel-Allison had clearly invested in me, and that would continue as I assumed more responsibility at the plant. GM had regularly sponsored classes and training since I started in 1972, but I had mastered most of those, so my next step was to complete my MBA. Each semester, I spent one week in residency, and then we met alternating Fridays and Saturdays for two years. It was an exciting time, and I found myself in classrooms with a diverse group of professionals from other companies, and it broadened my understanding of business. The lectures were terrific; there was a strong focus on collaboration and new technologies, and I saw this as another way to avoid becoming irrelevant or outdated.

The same year that I started my MBA, in 1984, I was promoted to plant manager, with more than two thousand people reporting to me. This promotion put me in an elite group that had access to the executive cafeteria—I had arrived on Mahogany Row. I did not realize how important it was to have access to such a facility until I walked through that door. There were nine codes, or levels, at the plant, and executives were called "no codes," which meant they surpassed the other levels. Breaking into that elite group was intimidating, so Bob Brown offered to go with me on the first day. I was nervous and expecting some resentment—I was sure somebody would think, "Why the hell is this black guy in our cafeteria?" If they were thinking that, nobody told me or acted as if I did not belong.

But the problem was real, and still is. Even today, you can find dozens of articles in places like *Fortune* magazine that address the issue. In a 2016 article, "Leading While Black: An Inside Look at What's Keeping Black Men Out of the Executive Suite," author Ellen McGirt recounts the story of Bernard J. Tyson, who in 1992 was named administrator of one of Kaiser Permanente's newest hospitals, in Santa Rosa, California. His colleague, Dr. Richard Stein, became a reluctant partner, and they were constantly at odds with each other. Tyson explained, "It was the most difficult relationship I ever had." Then one day, Stein invited Tyson to take a walk, and Stein opened up: "I have to confess something to you, something that might end our relationship. I never worked with a black man like this." Stein meant that he had never had a black peer, and this was 1992. Reflecting on that moment, Tyson explained, "It was at that moment I realized that the majority of the population doesn't have any sort of mental road map for how to relate to and work with someone different than themselves." I saw myself when reading that story. I started at GM two decades before Tyson's story took place, and most of my colleagues and peers had never even spoken to a black man as an equal and certainly had not been supervised by one.

But here I was, thirty-four years old, with twelve years at the plant. I was proud of my work and felt I had achieved some success, but I never dreamed that I would have crossed this invisible threshold. I had reached the top levels of management and soon realized that the executive cafeteria was more than a place to eat lunch—it was a place to do business, a place to cultivate lifelong friendships, and a place to chart my course forward. I had conversations there that I could not have anywhere else. There was a camaraderie that comes from shared experience and shared goals. I had finally, as my mother might say, arrived. But most importantly, I did not let anybody but me determine whether I belonged. That lesson would become critical to my success.

CHAPTER 7
THE BUYOUT

*"A jet engine business in what
is basically a car company is
not necessarily a good fit."*

B Y THE MID-1980s, General Motors Corporation had three divisions operating in Indianapolis: Allison Gas Turbine, Allison
Transmission Division, and the Truck and Bus Group Manufacturing Plant. With thousands of employees in the state, GM was,
according to an October 1988 article in *Indiana Business*, "central
Indiana's largest employer" along with Eli Lilly and Company, Kro-
ger, Indiana Bell Telephone, Ford Motor Company, the Associated
Group, L. S. Ayres and Company, Banc One Indiana Corporation,
Indianapolis Power and Light Company, and Thomson Consumer
Electronics Incorporated. The two Allison divisions contributed
nearly $1 billion to the state's economy through payroll and supplier
purchases.

I had worked for Detroit Diesel-Allison—which was formed on
September 1, 1970, as a result of a merger between Allison and Detroit Diesel—since 1972. On September 1, 1983, the year before I
was promoted to gear plant manager, the gas turbine division separated from Detroit Diesel-Allison and became Allison Gas Turbine
Division under general manager Dr. F. Blake Wallace. The company
manufactured gas turbine engines and components for aircraft, industrial, and marine uses, and it was one of the largest gear manufacturers in North America. From 1984 to 1993, I held a number
of positions with increasing levels of responsibility—area manager

of quality, chief of the material review board, manager of the gear plant, manager of helicopter engine assembly, general superintendent of manufacturing, inspection, quality, and finally special projects manager under Wilson Burns, who was the president of manufacturing operations. I was fortunate to grow in each position under Wallace's leadership.

Wallace was a genius in the industry and a terrific leader. He began his engineering career at California Institute of Technology, earning his degree in mechanical engineering in 1965 and completing his doctorate at Arizona State University two years later. He had broad experience, having worked on gas turbines for Pratt and Whitney, Garrett AiResearch, and General Electric. He was brought to Indiana to lead Allison, which was then a division of GM's Power Products and Defense Operations Group, and his great strength was hiring and developing talent.

Under Wallace, the company made serious inroads into the military engine market and focused on the fighter jet marketplace that had been mainly dominated by General Electric and Pratt and Whitney. In an article on "Allison's Seventy-Fifth" by Patrick McKeand, Wallace explained that "to get into the fighter jet engine business, we feel we must incorporate a big step forward in terms of technological advancements built into our engines. We've been working on that for the last five years. In that time, we won more engine technology development contracts from the government than any other engine manufacturer. As each of these technologies advance and we integrate them to finally produce an engine for the government, we will be a real contender." Allison launched the T800 helicopter engine at 1,300 horsepower. The U.S. Navy selected Allison's 6,000 shaft horsepower class turboshaft T406 engine to power its V-22 Osprey, which could take off and land like a helicopter and convert to a high-speed turboprop airplane capable of high-altitude flight. Another important contract was with a division of Allied Signal Aerospace Company to design and produce an engine for the army's RAH-66 Comanche.

The 1980s and 1990s were a period of profound change for both Allison and General Motors. On December 7, 1987, the transmission operations broke apart from the company and became Allison Transmission Division under Robert M. Clark, a thirty-five-year veteran of General Motors. The recession that hit the nation in 1990 and 1991 rippled through the company. GM lost $2 billion the first year, and $4.45 billion the second. The dramatic losses prompted the company to evaluate the subsidiaries that were not part of its core operations. So it came as no surprise in January 1992 that GM announced that it would sell Allison Transmission as part of a broad restructuring plan. This impacted 5,900 workers in Indianapolis. The year before, GM entertained a management buyout, but the bid the team submitted was not high enough, so by early 1992, it was put back up for sale. The proposed sale did not directly affect Allison Gas Turbine, but it certainly unsettled the broader community.

Through the spring and summer of 1992, GM received and rejected three offers for the turbine division. By this time, Allison Gas Turbine had three major product lines: light helicopter engines, big turboprop jet engines, and light industrial engines. Defense work accounted for about 40 percent of our business, something that was expected to decline by 25 percent over the next decade. New products were profitable, but it often took three to five years to bring them to market, and the start-up costs were often half a million dollars for a new engine. But we were an innovative company that was at the forefront of the industry in terms of technical capability, manufacturing expertise, and equipment. If evaluated as a stand-alone company, Allison Gas Turbine was estimated to rank four hundredth among the Fortune 500 companies, with sales of nearly $1 billion annually, but that was less than 1 percent of GM's business. Robert W. Hall, a professor at Indiana University School of Business, where I completed my MBA, was quoted as saying in the *Indianapolis Business Journal* on April 13, 1992, "A jet engine business in what is basically a car company is not necessarily a good fit."

This was an uncertain time throughout the Midwest and the nation—there were dozens of articles about GM downsizing and the perils of economic change. The *Indianapolis Star* published an article on November 15, 1992, entitled, "GM Slims Down: The Peril and Promise of Change at Indiana's Largest Employer." In the article,

Bill Koenig tells the story of Phil Hexamer, whose great-grandfather worked for GM in the 1920s along with six of his sons. They all referred to GM as "Generous Motors," for the stable, high quality jobs and benefits they provided. Robert M. Clark, who managed Allison Transmission, explained: "We look upon our jobs at General Motors and benefits and pay as a birthright. But in reality, job security is an earned right. You have to earn it every day." But much changed in the intervening decades. By 1991, GM employed 43,000 people in Indiana, down from 60,000 in the 1970s. The impact did not simply affect GM employees, it was felt by suppliers and other businesses that came to depend on the company. The sale of Allison Transmission to Germany's ZF Friedrichshafen was ultimately blocked by the Justice Department in November 1993, two years after the possible sale was announced. Uncertainty and soured labor relations prompted Robert Clark to step down in December 1993.

This was also a time of great change for my family. The boys graduated from Cathedral High School in 1990 and elected not to follow in our footsteps and go to college in the South. Instead, they chose the University of Dayton, two hours east of Indianapolis. Roderick knew he wanted to be a doctor from the time he was a child, but Broderick wanted to study the law. At the end of his sophomore year, Broderick changed his major to premed and went to summer school at Butler University to take some courses to catch up to Roderick. In their junior year at Dayton, the twins were both accepted to the University of Cincinnati College of Medicine. Evelyn continued teaching in Wayne Township but struggled with the boys' departure for college. They had always been close, and she was definitely experiencing a fierce case of empty nest syndrome. The boys were aware of her discomfort and made regular trips home.

In the summer of 1992, my parents came to visit us for the Fourth of July weekend. The boys came home from college to visit their grandparents. We had been talking for some time about the possibility of them moving to Indianapolis to be close to our family. After dinner on July 3, my mother complained about having painful stomach cramps. At first, she just thought something she ate did not agree with her or she had a bad case of gas, but we took her to the hospital as a precaution. After the doctors ran several tests, we were given devastating news—she had advanced pancreatic cancer. I immediately made an appointment with Dr. McCallam, my physician who had been so helpful to me over the years, just to have someone to talk to. I always trusted his judgment and knew that he would tell me the truth. And he did—I learned that the median survival rate from diagnosis to death for advanced pancreatic cancer was three and a half months. I expected bad news but not such a dramatic prognosis, and I burst into tears. Roderick and Broderick, who were now sophomores at the University of Dayton, joined me for the visit and had never seen me so emotional, and I think it really scared them.

My mother stayed in Indianapolis for a while and did some treatment, but it was really too late for it to be effective. In September, she returned to Florida, and she died the next month. I was devastated. All I had ever wanted to do in my life was to please and take care of my mother. She was my motivation, and making her proud was very important to me. Now she was gone, and I felt unmoored. Evelyn, the boys, and a number of close friends at work, like Wilson Burns, Billy Wright, Dennis Sumpter, and Ernie Vaughn, helped me cope with the loss. But the grief of losing a parent is like nothing I had ever experienced.

The funeral was a bit of a blur. We selected East Florida Primitive Baptist Temple because it could accommodate the crowds, and I remember the service was only about thirty minutes. I was heartened to see how many people from around the country came to Fort Pierce to support our family—friends, work colleagues, people of all colors and backgrounds showed up—because they knew I needed the support. I remember something that Mr. Little, who had been a mentor to me as a young man, said to me as we were leaving the church, "Lee, your mother is smiling down on you from heaven. She was so proud of you, and don't you ever forget that." After losing my mother, Evelyn and I felt we all needed a change of scenery, so we started to think about building our dream home. That would not be the only change we would experience.

My high school picture at Lincoln Park Academy, 1966. *Courtesy of Lee Rhyant*

Evelyn Louise Ingram at Lincoln Park Academy, 1966. *Courtesy of Evelyn Rhyant*

Posing with Evelyn, my high school sweetheart, 1967. *Courtesy of Evelyn and Lee Rhyant*

Working at Detroit Diesel-Allison in Indianapolis, 1973. *Courtesy of Lee Rhyant*

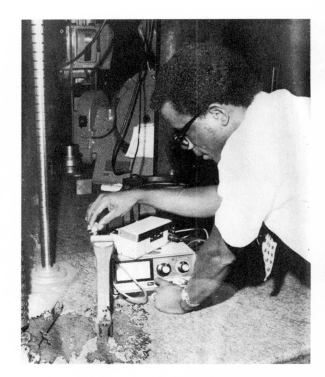

With Peter Joseph at Detroit Diesel-Allison, ca. 1973. *Courtesy of Lee Rhyant*

Family portrait, ca. 1977.
*Courtesy of Evelyn and
Lee Rhyant*

As a supervisor at Detroit Diesel-Allison, ca. 1980s. *Courtesy of Lee Rhyant*

My parents, Harding and Evelyn Rhyant, ca. 1980s. *Courtesy of Lee Rhyant*

With my parents at my MBA graduation, Indiana University, May 10, 1986. *Courtesy of Lee Rhyant*

With Roderick, Broderick, and Evelyn, 1991. *Courtesy of Evelyn and Lee Rhyant*

Roderick and Broderick's medical school graduation, University of Cincinnati, 1998. *Courtesy of Evelyn and Lee Rhyant*

Evelyn and I with Tony Bennett at an event in Indianapolis, November 20, 1999. *Courtesy of Lee Rhyant*

Visiting my hometown, Sasser, Georgia, 2002. *Courtesy of Evelyn Rhyant*

With our family, 2002. *Courtesy of Evelyn and Lee Rhyant*

Coretta Scott King, Evelyn, Alyce and Bill Sarno, and I at the Martin Luther King Jr. celebration in Atlanta, 2003. *Courtesy of Evelyn and Lee Rhyant*

Dexter King, Shan Cooper, and I at the Martin Luther King Jr. celebration, 2004.
Courtesy of Evelyn Rhyant

George Bush's inaugural ball, 2005. *Courtesy of Lockheed Martin*

With Evelyn, 2007. *Courtesy of Evelyn and Lee Rhyant*

With Jamie Foxx at the Morehouse College celebration in Beverly Hills, 2008. *Courtesy of Evelyn Rhyant*

On the line at
Lockheed Martin
in Marietta, 2007.
*Courtesy of Lockheed
Martin*

With Sam Olens and
Japanese business
leaders, March 25,
2008. *Courtesy of
Lockheed Martin*

Lincoln Park Academy, reunion, Atlanta, July 19, 2008. *Courtesy of Lee Rhyant*

Named 2009 National Management Association's Executive of the Year. *Courtesy of Lee Rhyant*

Receiving an honorary doctorate from Bethune-Cookman University, 2009.
Courtesy of Evelyn Rhyant

Groundbreaking ceremony for the Lee Rhyant Residential Center, Bethune-Cookman,
October 22, 2009. *Courtesy of Evelyn and Lee Rhyant*

City of Daytona Beach proclamation, October 22, 2009, on the naming of the Lee E. Rhyant Living & Learning Center. *Courtesy of Lee Rhyant*

With my successor, Shan Cooper, in a c-130 at Lockheed Martin in Marietta, 2011. *Courtesy of Lockheed Martin*

Speaking at Bethune-Cookman commencement, Fall 2012. *Courtesy of Evelyn Rhyant*

With Earl Little and Evelyn, 2012.
Courtesy of Evelyn and Lee Rhyant

Lee and Evelyn Rhyant with
Carol Strange Taggert and
Terry Fletcher, 2016. *Courtesy
of Lee Rhyant*

With Brianna Garney,
Roderick, Evelyn, Shaday
Word-Daniels, and Jahi
Word-Daniels, 2016.
Courtesy of Dennis Marrow

Roderick McLean, Vice President of the Air Mobility and Maritime Systems and Marietta Site General Manager at Lockheed Martin in Marietta, was given the 2011 Lee E. Rhyant Leadership Award. *Courtesy of Lockheed Martin*

With Dr. Kathy Schwaig and Lisa Duke at the KSU Coles College Hall of Fame Induction, 2016. *Courtesy of Dennis Marrow*

With Catherine Lewis and Dennis Marrow working on *Soaring*, 2021.
Courtesy of Camden Anich

With Kat Schwaig, the interim president of Kennesaw State University, 2021.
Courtesy of Jason Getz

In December 1993, Allison Gas Turbine was purchased by New York–based investment firm Clayton, Dubilier, and Rice (CDR) for $310 million—formally ending Allison's sixty-four-year history with GM. When I started at GM in 1972, I could have never imagined that they would have sold any of their subsidiaries. When you hired in at GM, there was a shared belief that your job would last forever. Though it was not a total surprise, when the buyout was announced, a lot of people were overwhelmed by uncertainty. They felt they had been betrayed by the company that had given them a sense of stability for so many decades. For many, GM was the only employer they had ever known. One major issue was retirement. Nonunionized salaried workers with less than thirty years at GM, which included me, saw drastic changes to their retirement plans. I had worked twenty-two years, and my GM retirement was frozen, so I moved from a pension system to a defined retirement program, what we now know as a 401(k), which was no longer managed by GM. Unionized workers, still represented by the UAW, did not see any major changes. Other benefits changed, and there was a clear sense that in moving to an independent company, the employees were headed into uncharted territory.

With the risk also came rewards. CDR had a track record for helping subsidiaries of large companies become stand-alone businesses, and they orchestrated a management buyout. As CDR president Joseph L. Rice III explained in the March 1994 issue of *Indiana Business Magazine*: "In our transactions, managers of the business invest their capital to own a significant share of the new company's common stock. We will offer 120 employees an opportunity to buy shares. The remainder of our salaried people will be owners by way of a 401(k) program. In the future, we'll consider a plan to give some form of ownership to the hourly people. Frankly, we want everybody to feel like they have a stake in the business, not just job security and pride . . . but ownership." The move prompted immediate calls for cost cutting to promote efficiency among the 4,400 employees.

Allison's chairman and chief executive officer, Blake Wallace, who had been with the company for eleven years, was quoted in a December 3, 1993, article in the *Indianapolis Star*: "What was good enough in the past won't be good enough for the future." Company profits had been reduced for several years because of the high research and development outlays, but there was an incentive to succeed. Managers of the company were given a 10 percent stake in Allison Engine, as Wallace explained: "We're betting our careers and our personal savings. Now the excuse is gone. We're no longer part of GM." The company's new ownership offered some powerful incentives—salaried workers were offered $2,000 bonuses, and a new bonus system was developed that was more strongly tied to performance. Long-term managers that helped shape my career—Wilson Burns, Frank Verkamp, and Mike Hudson—became executive vice presidents. Between them, they had eighty-nine years of experience with the company.

I was surprised when several key members of the management team approached me to join the buyout. About twenty top managers were included, and I was the only African American among that group. I was given an opportunity to purchase shares that made me a partial owner; the profits would then be divided among this group of twenty based on individual investment. I had given more than twenty years to this company and was proud to see that my sweat equity meant something. My value had been recognized, and I was being rewarded. I also saw my role in a whole new light. For the first time in my life, I was not an employee but an owner, so I had to start thinking like one. I became keenly interested and invested in financial issues and began participating in strategic meetings with the other owners focused on labor relations, contracts, inventory, shipping, and revenue. The financial training I had completed while at GM and my MBA became critical assets during this period, and I came to see that my success was tied directly to the company's success. This reality gave me a renewed commitment to my job.

Finalizing the management buyout was a big relief, but it was not without its casualties. Nearly five hundred hourly workers, many of whom worked on component lines that supplied other GM divisions, were terminated. We had several very unsettling years and were pleased to see the company remain intact and in Indianapolis. We were able to keep the management team together and retain a strong sense of loyalty among the hourly workers who remained. The change in the company was noticeable, as Wallace explained in a March 1994 article, "Allison Takes Off," published in the *Indiana Business Magazine*: "It is a little different to look at your cash flow instead of being managed by big, old GM. The opportunity to run a business differently and better is extremely good. In the near term, we simply have to be more efficient and look at cash differently, look at it as our money. We no longer have to ask somebody outside 'May I do this?' The decisions are made quickly and locally. We are decentralizing and delegating responsibility from down to what we call 'small business units.' We have to drive the decision-making process deep into the organization."

But our time as an independent company was short-lived. In 1995, Allison Engine Company was again purchased, this time by Britain's Rolls-Royce PLC for $525 million. Despite the name, the new owner was not part of the luxury auto brand but was instead the third largest global producer of aircraft engines. At first, the employees had mixed feelings about the change. There was some excitement about joining a large, well-respected company. That was tempered by concerns about how Allison's culture would integrate into a British-owned company, but the hope was that because Rolls-Royce focused exclusively on engines, there would be a shared language among the employees. The owners had additional worries, but when the sale was set at $525 million, the value of our stock increased dramatically.

We were renamed and placed in the Rolls-Royce Aerospace Division with the purpose of performing defense-related research, design, and development work for the government agencies. Our main client was the Department of Defense, and the company was structured to adhere to DOD security requirements, separate from the parent company. A year after we joined Rolls-Royce, in September 1996, Rolls-Royce Allison announced work on the Adour F405 engines to be used in the U.S. Navy's T045 Goshawk training planes. Allison also manufactured turbine blades, gears, and other parts for the Rolls-Royce RB211 engine, work that had been previously outsourced. In 1997, Rolls-Royce Allison received two major contracts from Lockheed Martin and AMR Eagle (part of American Airlines). Lockheed's $500 million contract was for the AE2100D2 turboprop engine that was used for the new C-27J Spartan aircraft. AMR's order was valued at $275 million and was for the AE 3007A1 engine for the 42EMB-145 Embraer regional jets.

Rolls-Royce also continued the model started by CBD during the management buyout, creating manufacturing cells—teams that do multiple tasks. In 1988, Rolls-Royce was reorganized into thirteen market-based units that were fairly autonomous—they did everything from research and development to production and marketing. Rolls-Royce Allison became home to three of those units: corporate and regional airlines, helicopters, and Defense North America. Mike Hudson became president of Rolls-Royce Allison and oversaw the helicopter and Defense North America units. John Ferry, executive vice president, would head up the corporate and regional airline business unit. Manufacturing efficiency became a key focus of the company. Rolls-Royce developed a series of significant goals— notably reducing the factory space by half. In doing so, the company could move operations that are housed in rented off-site spaces to the main headquarters. This was a lot of change in a short time. One of my main concerns was seeing how Allison was going to be integrated into the rest of Rolls-Royce. We had been part of a big company before, and everyone was curious what the restructuring would mean.

When the sale to Rolls-Royce was announced, many of the salaried employees were uneasy—here was another major change in less than two years. We had built a strong leadership team under the management buyout, and there was a palpable concern that Rolls-Royce might compromise the innovative culture that had been cultivated under Blake Wallace. Our concerns were quickly alleviated, and we found Rolls-Royce to be very welcoming. During my five years there, from 1995 to 2000, I held three positions: general superintendent of manufacturing inspection, vice president of quality, and vice president of production operations. Just like at GM, as my responsibilities increased, I was regularly sent for additional training and accepted temporary assignments. I regularly traveled to the United Kingdom and learned about negotiating global contracts, international trade, and shipping.

I also appreciated the culture at Rolls-Royce—high standards balanced with a tolerance for mistakes. I recall once when I was giving a presentation to John Rose about a project, and all of my charts were out of order. He was clearly frustrated with my careless mistake but did not embarrass me in front of the other staff. He met with me afterward to discuss it; he was not trying to shame me but genuinely seeking to help me see what I had done wrong and avoid repeating it. He reminded me that failure was not fatal; it is a natural part of the job, but you have to come to understand the role you play in that failure and remediate effectively. The three-person leadership team at Rolls-Royce, John Rose, Colin Green, and John Ferry, brought unique expertise in manufacturing, operations, and finance. Just as I had during my early years as a supervisor at GM, I found myself studying their methods, hoping to gain wisdom from them. During the management buyout, I also learned to accept responsibility for the company and found ways to ensure that my performance was constantly adding value.

Security clearances had become a regular way of life in my work, and this did not change at Rolls-Royce. Security clearances, granted by the U.S. government and governed by federal law, are used to certify that someone can be trusted with sensitive information. Just like at General Motors, we worked on a number of experimental programs for the Department of Defense, which always brought an additional layer of complexity. There were generally three clearance levels: confidential, secret, and top secret. In addition to clearances, individuals may be granted additional access for special compartmented information (SCI) or a special access program (SAP). It is expensive to get and maintain clearances, and the company that hired the employee had to fund them. The process was intrusive, as it should be. Your entire life is put under a microscope. Your financial records are scrutinized, every employer you ever had is interviewed, and government agents come to your house and talk to your family, friends, and neighbors. You could compromise your security clearance in a number of ways—for talking about "black programs" (secret programs that were not known by the public), for engaging in insider trading, or for financial problems such as bankruptcies that might make you vulnerable to blackmail. Training was essential in this area, and the entire workforce at Rolls-Royce was scrutinized at a level that I had not yet experienced. You not only had to pass an initial clearance but also had to constantly protect and monitor it. I was regularly reviewing policies related to confidentiality and the importance of not divulging sensitive information to outside sources. At Rolls-Royce, I had reached the point where I was not able to talk about my job with anyone—not family nor friends.

There were very real consequences for security breaches—the lives of our military servicemen and women and their families could be compromised. This was not a game, and while Rolls-Royce encouraged employees to remediate mistakes, there was no gray area when it came to security. There were real consequences—losing one's job and even jail. I knew colleagues who were not discrete, betrayed military secrets, and were tried as white-collar criminals. Espionage was a real problem, as was intellectual property theft. These stories rarely made the news because the companies who were engaged in this kind of highly sensitive work would have to reveal the nature of that work, which was not an option.

I loved my work at Rolls-Royce but was regularly approached by headhunters to plan my next step. I had been with Allison since 1972, and it was time to consider a change. I turned a number of opportunities down, but in 2000 I was made an offer that I could not refuse—taking the helm of Lockheed Martin Aeronautics Company's (LMAC) operations in Marietta, Georgia. With the boys off at school, Evelyn and I had been contemplating returning to the South for some time. The offer to help lead one of the nation's largest defense contractors was certainly appealing. I would oversee a company that was a powerful economic asset and that had a reputation for supplying the armed forces with mechanized muscle on a global scale. But it had its own unique set of challenges. Employment at the Marietta plant had dwindled to seven thousand, following a 20 percent work reduction. I would become the fifth chief executive in six years, and two days after I accepted the position, eleven workers filed a racial discrimination suit with the U.S. District Court in Atlanta. I was in for a rocky start and had to lean on my guiding principles to get me through.

CHAPTER 8
A ROCKY ROAD

*"I was willing to listen and make
changes when I could, but my main
focus was on dignity and respect."*

IN 1995, THE STOCKHOLDERS in Lockheed (America's second-largest defense contractor) and Martin Marietta (the nation's third largest) approved a $10 billion merger to create Lockheed Martin Corporation, with headquarters in Bethesda, Maryland. The new company would be the nation's largest military contractor—with $23 billion in annual revenues and 170,000 employees. The Georgia operation was renamed Lockheed Martin Aeronautical Systems Company (LMASC) and focused on aerospace engineering and missile technology. In 2000, I was hired as the first African American executive to oversee Lockheed Martin's Georgia operations in the midst of rumors of plant closings, budget cuts, and racial and labor unrest.

LMASC's story begins in 1942, during World War II, with the arrival of the Bell Aircraft Corporation (known as Bell Bomber), which would become Georgia's largest aircraft manufacturing facility. The *Atlanta Constitution* reported on February 25 of that year that Marietta became caught up in a "flurry of boomtime excitement and expansion." The 4.2 million square foot plant, positioned on forty-six acres, opened on April 15, 1943, at a cost of $73 million. During the war, Bell built 663 B-29 Superfortresses, which were long-range bombers designed by Boeing. More than 28,000 men and women were employed during the war, and the plant became a major economic engine for Marietta and Cobb County, about twenty miles from downtown Atlanta. New subdivisions were built, along with new facilities for water, sewer, and electricity. Marietta's city limits expanded.

In 1945, when the U.S. War Department no longer needed the aircraft, the contract was canceled, and Bell ceased operations in the state. The U.S. government used the Marietta plant for the next five years to store machine tools until the outbreak of the Korean War (1950–1953). In 1951, the California-based Lockheed Corporation agreed to reopen the plant and built the c-130, which served as a transport plane for troops and equipment that could take off on short, dirt runways.

The c-141 Starlifter, a transport plane double the size of the c-130, was both designed and built at the plant, and it transformed both the company and the state. In 1961 President John F. Kennedy announced a contract for 132 c-141s, and this decision played a significant role in helping address the problem of segregation in employment. The public nature of the contract brought to light that Lockheed operations in California were desegregated, while those in Georgia were not. The NAACP demanded a cancellation of the Georgia contract. On May 25, 1961, executives from Lockheed met with President Kennedy to sign the Plan for Progress, which he later called "a milestone for civil rights." The result was integration of assembly lines and hiring of black managers. The impact was swift and notable; one of Georgia's most visible and profitable employers was dismantling Jim Crow.

In 1965, Lockheed-Georgia signed a contract to build the c-5 Galaxy, twice as large as the c-141. The project was plagued almost from the beginning with cost overruns, errors, and Pentagon inflexibility, resulting in a quarter-billion-dollar loss for the company. The plane played a critical role in combat in both Vietnam (1964–1973) and Iraq (2003–2011) and helped expand the Lockheed-Georgia plant to 32,945 employees. On the heels of the c-5 Galaxy crisis, Lockheed invested in a passenger plane (the L-1011 Tri-Star) when Rolls-Royce, the engine manufacturer that I would eventually go to work for, filed for bankruptcy. Lockheed agreed to loan Rolls-Royce funds to keep the project alive but found few banks willing to take the risk. In August 1971, President Richard Nixon signed the Emergency Loan Guarantee Act to assure private banks that the government would subsidize the loan for companies who were deemed vital to national interest. Lockheed and Rolls-Royce both survived, and Lockheed eventually paid $31 million to retire the debt. These crises had a significant impact on the company; the labor force dropped from 33,000 in 1969 to 8,400 in 1977. Several military contracts during this time for additional c-141s and the c-5B helped stabilize the company.

The mid-1980s was an exciting time at Lockheed's aircraft division in Marietta. Don Melvin, writing for the *Atlanta Journal-Constitution* on June 23, 1995, explained, "With about 20,000 people hard at work, the floor of the main 3.5 million-square-foot plant was a hive of activity." But that all came crashing down with the fall of the Berlin Wall in November 1989 and the end of the Cold War. By the mid-1990s, when I first interviewed for a position at Lockheed, the workforce had been cut by half and a large portion of the plant stood empty. The post–Cold War period presented additional problems for other defense manufacturers as the government cut back on defense spending.

Norman R. Augustine, chairman and CEO of Lockheed Martin Corporation, explained this challenge in the May–June 1997 issue of *Harvard Business Review*, "The companies that make up the defense industry have seen more than 50 percent of their market disappear—a disaster not widely known by the public." After the Berlin Wall tumbled down, defense spending in the United States was dramatically cut. He goes on to explain, "The severity of the impact on the defense industry has been devastating, exceeding that of the great stock market crash of 1929 . . . only about one-quarter of the 120,000 companies that once supplied the Department of Defense still serve in that capacity; the others have shut down their defense lines of business or have dissolved altogether." Survival for these companies depended on their ability to combine with former competitors and create entirely new companies and markets. Augustine concluded that there are two kinds of companies, "those that are changing and those going out of business."

Augustine also argued that the "critical moment" for the industry came in 1993, when Les Aspin, then defense secretary, invited CEOs of major companies to the Pentagon for dinner and told them that within five years, half of them would be gone. The CEOs were faced with two difficult choices: try to move into new markets or increase market share in a declining industry. Success with either option required what Augustine called "external engineering" (merging companies) or "internal reengineering" (changing the way a company does business). In the rest of the *Harvard Business Review* article, Augustine detailed what Lockheed Martin did—from thwarting a hostile takeover in 1989 and 1990 to failing to buy Grumman in 1994 to consolidation (by purchasing General Electric's aerospace business and General Dynamics' space business). In sum, Lockheed Martin Corporation was comprised of seventeen once-independent entities, making them a "top provider to three government customers: the Department of Defense, the Department of Energy, and NASA." The article documents a number of other changes, but one approach stood out to me—be creative and step back far enough to take a critical look at all of your operations and put all solutions on the table. In the 1980s, NASA asked Lockheed Martin to cut the weight of a space shuttle fuel tank. The company assembled a team to study the problem and suggested using exotic materials to solve it. Finally, one of the employees suggested not painting it. That simple solution cut 800 pounds from the shuttle. Sometimes the simple answer is the right one.

The portion of Norman Augustine's article that resonated most with me was his mantra, "Remember that your assets go home at night." His focus on cultivating and investing time in employees and managers was the key to building a strong team. He also believed that bringing customers into the plant was important—be it a pilot who flew an airplane we built for the Gulf War or an astronaut who traveled on the space shuttle. I did something similar but with a focus on veterans. I learned that nearly 20 percent of my team had served in the armed forces. So I made sure at every meeting to begin by asking the veterans to raise their hands, and then I launched into a short speech, "We never want to forget who we are working for, the men and women in our armed forces—all of those who have served and are still serving. They are our customers, and they know better than anybody that freedom is not free." I regularly invited World War II veterans, including members of the famed Tuskegee Airmen, to visit, along with local and national political leaders, such as Senator Johnny Isakson and military brass. We hosted special Veterans Day and Memorial Day programs. Seeing how our work affected people's lives was a powerful lesson and kept us humble and committed to doing the best work we could.

Lockheed Martin Aeronautical Systems Company, the group I was about to lead, was one of Lockheed's two major units—California's operations focused on space and missiles and Marietta's operations focused on aircraft manufacturing. After the merger, the Marietta plant was working to "sweat the fat" out of its operation by contracting fire protection, printing, and auto maintenance; improving efficiency; targeting training to make workers more accountable for their work instead of depending on inspectors; and reducing inventory. But there were still a number of issues that needed attention, and I was brought in five years after the merger to address them.

My arrival in Marietta felt like a culmination of all of my twenty-eight years of hard work. All of the mentoring, all of the apprenticeships and special assignments, all of the leadership training, all that I had learned in the classroom and at the Allison plant prepared me to step into this new role. I truly felt that whatever was going to be thrown at me, I had seen it, fixed it, or had the expertise to handle it. I was not shocked by anything I learned about the company and took the helm at LMASC confident that I could lead it.

Lockheed interviewed me for a vice president of operations position in the mid-1990s, but the timing was not right. My father was ill and still living in Florida, and Evelyn was still teaching. The boys were in college nearby, and we were not ready to move. Five years later, another headhunter urged me to consider taking the helm of the Marietta plant. The boys were twenty-eight, had finished medical school, and were starting their careers. Evelyn and I had grown weary of the long, gloomy winters in Indiana and were thinking about moving to a warmer climate. My health was also causing me trouble. I had two surgeries on my prostate, surgery on my gallbladder, and a month before taking the helm at Lockheed, I had an extremely painful nasal surgery and was suffering from vertigo. I was fifty years old and felt like I had one more big job in me. If I was going to make a change, the time was now. I had several criteria for a new position—I wanted to stay in aerospace; I wanted to work for a respected company; and I preferred to be back in the South. Lockheed was a perfect fit.

When I made the decision to take the helm at Lockheed in Marietta, Rolls-Royce was very supportive. The two companies issued a joint news release, and I began working on the transition. Evelyn was still teaching, so we decided that I would move and she would continue with her career. She wanted to stay close to Broderick and Roderick and wanted to close out her career on her own terms in Indianapolis. This arrangement lasted for six years, and she regularly commuted between Indianapolis and Atlanta for visits and holidays. I initially thought I would remain at Lockheed a few years and then retire, so it did not make sense to uproot the entire family. This decision was born out of a promise I made my mother years ago.

When Evelyn and I married, my mother urged me to make sure that I gave my wife every opportunity to develop and nurture her own career, independent from me, even if that meant we could not always be together. I wanted her to have a whole life, not one that was determined exclusively by my job. I had a number of friends and colleagues whose wives sacrificed their dreams for the sake of their husbands' careers, much to their later regret. I did not want that to happen to us, so we sold the home and purchased a condominium close to her school. There were some problems with the builder, so she had to stay in an apartment on a temporary basis. Evelyn staying in Indianapolis a while longer turned out to be a great decision because our first grandchild, Zachariah, was born in March 2001, and being close by allowed her to thoroughly enjoy the role of doting grandmother.

In Atlanta, I moved into executive housing in Buckhead, six miles from the plant, and stayed there from July to November until Evelyn and I could decide on a longer-term solution. We finally bought a house in East Cobb, near Lassiter High School. At first we thought it would be a temporary solution while we built a home, but we soon fell in love with the neighborhood because it had so many young families and children.

On my first day of work, I was greeted by protesters. It was not entirely a surprise; there was a lot of conflict between workers and management at the plant. This was part of what I was hired to help resolve. There was a miniaction organized by the union on that first day, where workers walked through the plant complaining about discrimination and demanding respect for the union. I had been at GM for more than twenty years, so I understood what motivated them to make a bold stand on my first day. There were local television stations on hand to capture the events as they unfolded, and it made national news. It was disruptive, but it also gave me an honest view of the situation at the plant and a sense of the major issues I would need to address.

Marietta's problems were real, especially for African Americans, who comprised 800 of the 7,500 workers at the plant. They complained about the lack of promotions, working conditions, pay, vacation, and also the prevalence of racist graffiti portraying the Ku Klux Klan in bathrooms. I had seen some of the issues at the Allison plant in Indianapolis and was the target of some of them early in my career. There were several pending discrimination lawsuits, and in January 2000, an investigation by the U.S. Equal Employment Opportunity Commission (the same group that helped Evelyn years ago with her teaching position) found that white managers had discriminated against black employees who had more seniority and experience than white employees who were awarded promotions. Several other major high-profile companies, like Coca-Cola and Georgia Power, also were the subjects of similar suits during this period. The EEOC ultimately issued nearly a dozen findings of racial discrimination and one finding of bias against the disabled. Five months later, on May 11, 2000, eleven African American employees, the Workers Against Discrimination, filed a discrimination lawsuit in the U.S. District Court in Atlanta claiming bias and a hostile work environment. The case asked the court to allow two class action lawsuits, one for hourly and one for salaried employees at Lockheed plants from South Carolina to Texas. Workers reported having a hangman's noose and a "Back to Africa" ticket left on their workstations. The lead attorney for the workers, Josie Alexander, was quoted in a May 11, 2000, article in the *St. Louis Post-Dispatch*: "People should have a right to work without unlawful discrimination. And where there is discrimination that is so pervasive as the discrimination at Lockheed, and when a union refuses to stand up for the workers, there's a problem." Civil rights icon and congressman John Lewis, along with Congresswoman Cynthia McKinney, lent support to the effort. Johnnie Cochran, who gained fame in the O. J. Simpson case, joined the plaintiff's team. Two days later, I was named successor to Tom Burbage as the head of the Lockheed plant in Marietta.

As you can imagine, putting an African American at the helm raised some eyebrows. The lawyer suing Lockheed was quoted in a May 13, 2000, article of the *Atlanta Journal-Constitution*, "Merely replacing the site manager at one plant won't compensate mistreated workers or prevent future occurrences." Sam Grizzle, the spokesman for the Marietta plant, countered, "Lee was selected for this position on solid qualifications as a manager and leader in manufacturing operations. His race had nothing to do with the move. We hope anything we do here has a positive effect, but this wasn't done because of the lawsuit." I had reporters—both local and national—ask me the same basic question over and over again: "You have come to work for this racist company, and you are black. How do you square that?" My reply was always, "I'm here to fix it, and if my team at Lockheed can't fix it, I'll join the other side."

As Randall Patton documents in the epilogue of his book *Lockheed, Atlanta, and the Struggle for Racial Integration*, *Reid v. Lockheed* did not make it to trial, and it was not settled. He explained, "U.S. district judge J. Owen Forrester denied the EEOC's petition to join the case in January 2001, and on August 2, he ruled that the charges contained in the multilocation lawsuit did not constitute a class action. Individual plaintiffs were free to continue their cases separately, but the tenor of the judge's ruling and the difficulty and expense of proceeding in this manner made such a course unattractive."

But race was not the only issue. I was the fifth plant chief in six years—that kind of turnover makes it nearly impossible to create stability. I arrived just as the plant was completing layoffs of 2,800 workers, which reduced the workforce to 7,000, heightening the sense of uncertainty. There had also been a reduction in orders for the c130J cargo plane and a fair amount of uncertainty about the F-22 fighter program. The Marietta plant was also still grappling with the consolidation, which put it under the leadership of Dain Hancock, who headed Lockheed Martin Aeronautics Company in Fort Worth, Texas. Tom Burbage, whom I replaced, became executive vice president of that new unit. Terry Graham, who was Tom's second in command, retired as chief operating officer, and that position was not going to be filled. So the day-to-day operations fell squarely in my lap.

The union was also a big issue that needed attention. They faced the same problems I had seen at GM, and I had witnessed plenty of posturing and distrust that creates the adversarial environment between workers and management. During my tenure, there were strikes, contract disputes, and constant conversations about workers' rights. The International Association of Machinists and Aerospace Workers (IAM), Local Lodge 709, was the union that represented our hourly workers, and I understood their role. I learned early on to steer clear of union politics and not to try to manipulate the process; that was a recipe for disaster. I was willing to listen and make changes when I could, but my main focus was on dignity and respect. A number of issues that the plant had grappled with were fairly easy to fix—honoring shift preferences, keeping the restrooms clean, providing affordable and tasty food in the cafeteria, and negotiating contracts in good faith. I also encouraged my leadership team to participate in union-sponsored events, such as walkathons, to show solidarity with our employees. I learned early on in my career that you can eliminate a lot of conflict by simply being respectful and fixing small problems before they become major issues.

In this environment I felt that I had to demonstrate in a public way that things were going to change. In order to convey this message, I scheduled about seventy breakfasts at the plant for about ten people each time. Anyone could sign up—it was first come, first served. I never asked for a list of who was going to attend, and at each breakfast, I talked about my background, encouraged the participants to tell me their stories, and we brainstormed about how to improve the plant. If issues of race or the lawsuits came up, I usually said some version of this speech: "I hear you, and I care about these issues. I cannot speak about the past, because I was not here and do not know all the details. But I can guarantee you that I will not tolerate bad behavior from anyone on our team. The lawsuits will follow their own course in the courts, but along with my management team, I am determined to help eliminate what has clearly become a toxic environment. I have a lot to learn, and I will work with hourly employees, contractors, the union, and management to help bring about a culture change." I would always have a member from the facilities team at the breakfast, and if there was something that could be easily fixed, we would try to do it that day. The bathrooms were a constant source of friction, largely because of the racially and sexually explicit graffiti that seemed to appear daily. Jack Lambert, the head of human resources in Marietta, started inspecting the restrooms every weekend and had a team clean them and remove the graffiti. A few months of this kind of monitoring seemed to send a message that we were not going to tolerate anything offensive and that we cared about professionalism and safety.

I thought that a public declaration of my values was important, but the work was going to be hard. I had been a supervisor on a shop floor, and I know how hard it is to change the culture, especially when you are trying to change hearts and minds. I was fortunate to have Jack Lambert at Lockheed. In my first weeks, he briefed me about issues ranging from favoritism to intentional and unintentional bias. One thing I learned from my mentors at GM was that an organization takes on the personality and values of its leaders. If the organization condones racism, sexism, and disrespect for the lowest-paid workers and the union, it is because the leader allows it. I loved President Harry Truman's aphorism—"a leader has to lead." Even though the rest of the quote references politics, it remains relevant for business. I knew I had to listen, but more importantly I had to be decisive and lead if I was going to get anywhere.

To tackle this diverse range of challenges, I devised a multiprong strategy. I sensed that the plant was on an upswing, otherwise I would not have taken the job. The c-130J's orders were beginning to come back in, and Lockheed decided the spring before I arrived that the F-22 assembly would not move to Texas. With that issue settled, I could focus on making the plant cost competitive and efficient. Early in my tenure, we did a major review of the plant. This included organizational charts, business processes, and technical issues. I was determined to take Marietta from being a plant that Lockheed considered closing to a jewel in the company's crown. The first major step was to rebrand ourselves in the local community, which would, in turn, help rebrand the Marietta plant within Lockheed.

We had a lot of bad publicity to overcome. So my leadership team—including Hamilton Holmes, Shan Cooper, and Jack Lambert—joined me in an all-hands-on-deck approach. We went to Rotary and Kiwanis Club meetings, we met with high school students, fifth-grade STEM teachers, business leaders in Atlanta, and journalists and editors of local newspapers. We also met with Sam Olens of the Cobb County Commission and the Cobb Chamber. He was a strong advocate and was especially helpful during the strikes in 2002 and 2005. He worked hard to make sure that things among Lockheed, the city, and the county did not get ugly. Along with other business leaders, he promoted community programs that we supported, like walkathons, the Martin Luther King Jr. celebration, and other fundraisers. Our goal was to put a different face on the company—and we experienced a fair amount of hostility and distrust. But I was determined to turn this around. I knew Lockheed was a great company, and I did not want anyone to be embarrassed to work there. I valued our employees and our product, and I knew I had to show up and take my lumps. I was not sure for how long, but I was not going to give up.

My secret weapon became the African American pastors and community leaders, many of whom were giants in the civil rights movement. It was abundantly clear that they were going to be a key constituency, so I made myself available for dozens of closed-door conversations. The first meeting came by way of a phone call on my second day on the job. Pastor Earl Moore, a Seventh-day Adventist minister in Atlanta, had been helping to advise the internal group suing Lockheed. He was well educated, respected, and had a reputation for being tough. He called to ask if we could meet, and I agreed because I wanted to hear about the concerns of African American workers from a source outside of the company. I knew he would tell me the truth, and I got an earful about how Lockheed had let his community down. He helped coordinate a meeting with the Atlanta Concerned Black Clergy and individual sessions with community leaders Tim McDonald, Joe Beasley, Harris Travis, Winston Strickland, Andrew Young, John Lewis, Deanne Bonner, C. T. Vivian, and Dr. Joseph Lowery. These people were giants, and I took a half-day vacation so I could sit in a room and listen to men and women who had fought battles far greater than I ever did. They had a lot of questions for me and were very respectful. I think they just wanted to ensure that I would treat the African American employees no different than anybody else. At the end of our meeting, I told them how much I valued their input and that I would walk away from Lockheed if they did not have confidence in me. I tried to conduct myself in a humble but professional way, out of respect for what they had done, and I needed their support. I told them that I would be fair, but not everybody was going to be happy. Lockheed would sometimes make unpopular decisions, but they would not be based on race or discrimination.

Several of these men, including Dr. Lowery and Ambassador Andrew Young, made a trip to Bethesda to meet with the Lockheed leadership. They advocated for the African American community and wanted Lockheed to see how committed those employees were. I think our top brass was impressed and saw an aspect of that community that had been invisible to them. We also met with other stakeholders, like Winston Strickland, who was a Cobb County businessman who owned a restaurant and barber shop. He was a powerful force who advocated for the neediest among us—he met with juveniles who had been jailed, raised funds for youth programs, and was a constant voice for fairness. I used to pay him ten dollars for a haircut and tip him thirty dollars for the advice. I could always get the temperature of the African American community from him. Deanne Bronner, of the Cobb NAACP, and Shirley Franklin, the mayor of Atlanta, became powerful allies. Lockheed employees lived all over metro Atlanta, and Shirley understood more than anybody that our success reflected on the city.

I also had to build a strong foundation with the media. Bill Kinney and Otis Brumby of the *Marietta Daily Journal* could have destroyed my credibility, but we developed an honest and productive working relationship, and I felt Lockheed enjoyed fair coverage from their paper. Bill knew everybody in Cobb County, and he became someone I would call regularly for advice. Otis interviewed me on my first and last day on the job, and I told my wife upon his passing in 2012, the year after I left Lockheed, that he had some bullets that he could have shot my way but never did. With Cobb County business leaders, I met with editors of newspapers in Atlanta, Savannah, Columbus, Augusta, and other Georgia cities to help build our brand. Other business leaders, like Bob Moultrie and Earl Smith, understood that I would need allies, and they regularly provided assistance. Local and national political leaders also became confidants, such as Senators Saxby Chambliss and Johnny Isakson. Brian Johnson, our head of governmental affairs at Lockheed, facilitated meetings with Phil Gingrey (who represented Georgia's eleventh district), Cynthia McKinney (who represented Georgia's sixth district), and Bob Barr (who represented Georgia's seventh district).

The thing that saved me in the transition was that I had inoculated myself from undue influence. Evelyn and I purposely lived two or three levels below our means. During our entire careers, we saved and invested our money and were very frugal. We never got tangled up in complex financial schemes that sometimes ensnare public officials and thus steered clear of the need to ask for favors. We had fortified ourselves financially and focused on building strong relationships and honest reputations. That made it possible for me to speak candidly and address problems directly. We were not beholden to anybody. I did not grow up in Atlanta, and as a result did not have long-standing family or community relationships that needed to be tended. As my mother used to say, "I was not in nobody's ass pocket." That freedom would become one of the keys to my success.

CHAPTER 9
NINETY MINUTES

"Don't let this kill you."

NINETY MINUTES. That is how long it took Dain Hancock and me to board a plane bound for Meridian, Mississippi. I had been in a meeting on July 8, 2003, with Dain (executive vice president of Lockheed Martin Corporation and president of Lockheed Martin Aeronautics), James G. Roche (secretary of the air force), and John P. Jumper (his chief of staff) in Marietta, about twenty miles north of Atlanta. There were about forty of us in all—Lockheed executives, including my boss Ralph Heath, and air force and other government officials—talking about the F-22 Raptor, a single seat stealth tactical fighter aircraft developed for the air force. We were discussing how to get the program back on track and were about an hour into the meeting when Dain received an important phone call from Bob Elrod from Fort Worth. When he stepped out, my assistant called to tell me that there had been a racially motivated shooting at the Lockheed plant in Meridian. Dain came back into the room and told everyone what had happened. The meeting quickly adjourned, and he began making plans to fly to Mississippi. Sensing that I might be helpful, I scrambled to gather some personal belongings and joined him on the drive to Dobbins Air Reserve Base, where Dain's plane had been parked. We charted a course for Meridian and were met at the plant several hours later by Terry Powell (senior vice president for human resources for Lockheed).

Before we left, I called Dr. Joseph Lowery, Ambassador Andrew Young, the Reverend Jesse Jackson, and Pastor Earl Moore—all civil rights leaders with whom I had worked. They were no strangers to this kind of violence, and I thought I could benefit from their wisdom and advice as I prepared to make what I predicted would be a very difficult journey. What I remember most from those calls was how they prayed for me, knowing that I was going to need all the strength I could muster. Ninety minutes after Dain ended the meeting, we were on the plane to Meridian, a town of forty thousand. It was a short flight, and after landing, we drove to the Lockheed plant at 3017 Lockheed Drive.

The Meridian Lockheed plant began operation in August 1969 and initially produced the L-1011 jet airlines empennage (the tail assembly at the rear of an aircraft that provides stability during a flight). It soon expanded to producing aircraft components for the JetStar, the C-5 Galaxy and C-141 Starlifter strategic airlifters, P-3 Orion submarine hunter, F-22 Raptor fighter jet, and C-130J Super Hercules tactical airlifter. In Meridian, we were met at the airport by a security team from Lockheed, and they did their best to brief us on the thirty-five-minute drive to the plant. We peppered them with questions: What happened? Were there injuries? Who was the shooter? Was he still alive? What motivated him? They were dazed themselves and did not have all of the details but did know that a white employee targeted black coworkers, and on the morning of the shooting, 138 employees were working on the floor.

The local police had cordoned off the plant with yellow tape and were still gathering information when we arrived. They allowed us to enter, and we were quickly ushered upstairs so we could get a bird's-eye view of the shop floor, which was now a crime scene. Dain and I were both stunned by what we saw—there were puddles of blood everywhere, several dead bodies were still on the ground, and the plant was swarming with police. I remember glimpsing the body of a woman who had been shot and rushing down the hall to the bathroom to throw up. The scene was gruesome, but it was not just the violence that made me ill. That woman could have been my sister or my mother; she could have been any member of the black community who had been the victim of hatred and discrimination. The whole scene was terrible and senseless. I was surprised by how fast my horror turned to anger and frustration—about racism and about all the brutal things that I had witnessed in my lifetime. I felt the same way that I did on June 21, 1964, when I learned that James Chaney, Andrew Goodman, and Michael Schwerner were killed in Neshoba County, Mississippi. That was only an hour away from where we were now standing. I felt the same way that I did on April 4, 1968, when Dr. Martin Luther King Jr. was assassinated in Memphis. All of the fear, anger, and hate regurgitated in me, and I had to purge it out.

Dain was keenly aware that he and I were going to see this tragedy through completely different lenses, and he was very sensitive to allow me some time to process it from the perspective of an African American man who had grown up in the Jim Crow South. While he stepped out to call the leadership team at Lockheed and plan a response, I began to worry about the workers and their families. Some of them had not yet received the news of the shooting, and others were just finding out that their loved ones had been killed. It was a terrible moment, and time seemed to slow to a glacial pace. It took me a while to pull myself together, to get to a point where I could speak to people. But I knew I wanted to help and to find out what happened so I could help with the healing. We soon learned the details of that fateful morning.

Douglas Williams, a divorced father of two who had worked on the assembly line since 1984, attended a mandatory ethics and diversity class with thirteen colleagues in an annex building at the plant that morning. He stayed for only a few minutes before storming out saying: "Y'all can handle this." He told his supervisor, Jeff McWilliams, that he was "going to take matters into his own hands" and went to get a semiautomatic rifle and shotguns from his pickup truck. He raced back to the meeting wearing bandoliers full of extra shotgun shells at about 9:40 a.m., screaming, "I told y'all to stop fucking with me! Didn't I tell y'all not to fuck with me?" It was at that moment that he began shooting. His fellow employees hit the floor as bullets started flying around the room.

Mickey Fitzgerald tried to calm Williams down, and Williams shot him in the face; then Williams turned his gun on Sam Cockrell, whom he believed had made complaints about him. He wounded Al Collier in the back and right hand, followed by Charles Scott and DeLois Bailey. Steve Cobb, the plant manager, and Brad Bynum, Chuck McReynolds, and Brenda Dubose were all wounded by ricocheting bullets. Williams then left the room to look for Jack Johns, the production manager, before returning to target his fellow Lockheed employees. When he finally left the annex building, he raced to the main plant looking for fellow employees he believed had reported him to management for making racist threats. Pete Threatt tried to take his gun away but was unsuccessful. Williams shot five other people at point-blank range before killing himself. The shooting would be the deadliest workplace shooting since a software tester in Wakefield, Massachusetts, killed seven people at Edgewater Technology the day after Christmas three years earlier.

According to his colleagues, Williams had a history of making racial threats, so the shooting was not entirely surprising. Lynette McCall, who worked at the plant and was killed that day, told her husband, as reported in the *New York Times* on July 9, 2003, that the gunman was "going to come in one day and kill a bunch of niggers and then he was going to turn the gun on himself." Jarvis Towner, a coworker who was not wounded, recalled that Williams was one of "those kind of people" who would "go postal." The whole tragic incident took about nine minutes. Five of the six people who were killed in the shooting—DeLois Bailey, Sam Cockrell, Mickey Fitzgerald, Lynette McCall, Charles J. Miller, and Thomas Willis—were African American. Seven others were injured: Brad Bynum, Steve Cobb, Al Collier, Brenda Dubose, Chuck McReynolds, Henry Odom, Charles Scott, and Randy Wright.

The whole scene at the plant was chaotic, and a number of employees were standing around in a daze. Others had been taken to the hospital for evaluation. Family members had begun to arrive, and the police did a great job of coordinating the response. But it was difficult to determine who had been shot and learn anything about their condition. Workers were constantly approaching our team looking for someone to talk to—seeking some sense of normalcy. We knew that after we walked the floor and had a full briefing that we had to help lead the response. We decided to go to the hospital, to visit the families, and see what else we could do. Our reception there was mixed—some family members were glad to see someone from Lockheed, others poured their grief onto us and were angry and hysterical. There was no playbook or manual to guide anyone through this process. All we could really do was show up and do our best to help. I learned long ago that you cannot judge someone in the throes of an overwhelming tragedy—you just have to be present and listen. Most people just want to be heard. We stayed a few hours and then started working with our human resources team to develop a strategy and to get enough people on the ground to coordinate a response. The Holiday Inn became our headquarters, and each family that had an injured employee was assigned a support team.

We ultimately stayed for two weeks, and during that time I spent hours meeting with local African American ministers, community leaders, and social workers. I visited each family and attended every funeral. As the only African American executive from Lockheed, my role was unique. I had grown up in the South and felt comfortable offering my help. Segregation and racism were part of my lived experience, and I was able to express my sympathy and share my outrage with the affected families. The funerals were very emotional, and they reminded me of my grandmother's service when I was a child. I tried to arrive right as the service started so as not to distract the families. After one funeral, I saw a woman that I had visited in the hospital after her husband had been injured. She was understandably distraught that day and unloaded her rage on me. I understood, but it was very painful. At the service for one of the employees who had been killed, his spouse caught my eye and walked over and hugged me. I remember her saying in that embrace, "Don't let this kill you." I think she knew that this experience had transformed me. There was a part of me struggling with the fact that the fears from my childhood had come to fruition. I think many in the African American community in Meridian felt like I did—that Jim Crow and the accompanying racial violence had lessened. But it had not, and I felt the same outrage years later watching the news on June 17, 2015, after Dylann Roof shot congregants at the Emanuel African Methodist Episcopal Church in Charleston, South Carolina. I felt it again after watching the Unite the Right rally in Charlottesville, Virginia, on August 11 and 12, 2017.

As the head of the Lockheed Martin plant in Marietta, I also worked closely with the leadership of the Meridian plant to help bring it back online within a week of the shooting. It was a difficult process, partly because many of the workers were suffering from the shock of the event. But we all felt that trying to get the plant back in operation would be the best thing for everyone. On the day we reopened the plant, we held a service for the workers who had been lost or injured, and that seemed to start an ongoing healing process. Civil rights leaders came to Meridian and Lockheed executives offered support to the families. The long-term impact on the community was harder to gauge, but the shooting seemed to prompt a subtle shift. There was a coming together, with the white and black communities engaged in several hard conversations about race. It was long overdue and sad that it had to be prompted by a tragedy. There were a number of court cases after the shooting, and I participated in some very difficult depositions. Whatever the outcome, the affected families and broader community would never be the same.

Neither was I. The close and personal encounter with this kind of violence transformed me, and I found myself shaken. This all happened on the heels of my parents' deaths and my undergoing major surgery, which just added to the wear and tear of corporate life. I was also grateful for my family, my faith, my career, and my community, but I felt an undefinable pain. The shooting also forged a different relationship between me and the executive team of Lockheed. The company became more focused on preventing workplace violence, which has become so common today. It spurred a conversation throughout Lockheed about race and violence. It also forced me to think about my own team in Marietta and to question whether I had created an inclusive and safe environment for the men and women who worked for me. I walked away from Meridian with a renewed sense of duty—to do right by the people who walked through the doors every day. Was I doing everything I could to be fair, respectful, and provide opportunity? I spent a lot of time with my leadership team after the shooting discussing what we could do to help prevent such a tragedy. In the coming years, every new workplace shooting forced me to relive the tragedy at Meridian and recommit myself to safety for my colleagues.

The shooting did not derail my goals to make the Marietta plant not just profitable but a jewel in Lockheed's crown. The eleven years that I was at Lockheed was a time of profound change. I joined Lockheed in 2000 at a difficult time. A few years before I arrived, in 1998, slow sales of the c-120J airlifter raised fears of production shutdown. That next year, 2,000 jobs—20 percent of the total—were cut. In January 2000, another 800 jobs were cut under corporate reorganization, and three months later 100 machinist jobs were cut. When I arrived, we were still quelling rumors that the plant was closing and operations were moving to Texas. But new orders of the c-130J kept the production lines open. In 2001, Lockheed won the largest defense aerospace contract in history—a $200 billion contract to build the F-35, or Joint Strike Fighter, for the air force, navy, and marines. This made a huge difference, but it did not solve my major problem—infrastructure. My time at GM told me that if your systems and infrastructure are outdated, then you cannot remain competitive.

Labor issues were also a persistent issue. In 2002, 78 percent of members of the International Association of Machinists Local 709 at the Marietta plant rejected a three-year contract proposal that would have raised wages by 10 percent and offered a $1,000 signing bonus. Then 82 percent of the unionized workforce voted to strike, making it the first strike at the Marietta plant in twenty-five years. At 12:01 a.m., on March 11, workers began picketing at the plant's gates in Marietta. This was not simply a small, local labor dispute. Lockheed was the nation's largest defense contractor. A work stoppage anywhere disrupted operations everywhere. Union president Jim Carroll was quoted in the *Atlanta Journal-Constitution*: "Every member that votes for this proposal is voting to rob his brothers and sisters of their jobs. A raise isn't going to do you any good if they take away your job." The striking workers composed about a third of the Marietta plant's seven thousand employees, and I asked salaried employees to work on the assembly line. But I also demanded that the nonstriking employees respect those who chose to walk out. The strike at our plant was not an isolated incident—Lockheed was also in talks with unionized workers in Sunnyvale and Palmdale, California. The strike lasted forty-nine days, and I worked hard to ensure that communication between the leadership in Marietta and the union was respectful, frequent, and productive. I understood the union's perspective, and though I believed they could have resolved the issue without a strike, they did receive a good contract.

A second strike came just three years later, in March 2005. Rank-and-file members opposed union leaders and rejected a deal that was ratified by the International Association of Machinists Local 709, which represented about 2,800 workers in Marietta. The sticking point seemed to be health care and retirement benefits. I was respectful of the union position, but I also was concerned because the Pentagon had asked for deep cuts to the $72 billion Raptor program and wanted to end the Hercules program the following year. A striking union did not help our case when proposed budget cuts went to the heart of our core programs. Ultimately, the union ended up accepting Lockheed's original offer, a three-year deal that promised 10 percent wage increases and a $1,500 signing bonus. But they also accepted increases to health care and insurance premiums. The short strike progressed without any major conflict, and I was impressed with the level of professionalism, respect, and patience exhibited by all of our employees. I believe this allowed us to resolve our differences and keep the labor dispute from becoming long and protracted.

We enjoyed some real successes during my tenure, and in 2008, Lockheed was named the 2008 Georgia Manufacturer of the Year. We were thrilled with the honor, and it brought prestige and valida-

tion to the plant. That next year, I was named the National Manufacturing Association's Executive of the Year. I was shocked but truly
honored. Evelyn, Roderick and Broderick, and their wives, Anjulia
and Andrea, attended the banquet in New Orleans. It was such an
honor to share this with my family and with the whole Lockheed
team. But we did not have even a minute to rest on our laurels. We
constantly grappled with the ups and downs that come along with
manufacturing. The future of the F-22 was debated in 2009, and in
2010, the F-35 Lightning II center wing assembly came to Marietta.

By this point in my career, the boys had completed medical school,
married, and started their own families, and they were building
their own practices. Roderick moved to Atlanta, while Broderick remained in Indianapolis. In 2006, Evelyn had completed thirty-one
years in the public school system in Indianapolis and felt that it was
time for her to retire. We were blessed with three beautiful grandchildren—Zachariah, Jeremiah, and Gabriella—and had settled into
a pretty nice routine. Evelyn continued to travel between Indianapolis, Atlanta, and Fort Pierce, maintaining rich friendships and staying connected to family. In 2011, I decided it was the right time to
step down. *Georgia Trend* reported that same year that Lockheed
Martin was a vital force in Georgia's $3.4 billion aerospace industry.
We had 8,000 employees—or 10 percent of the state's aviation employees. I was proud of my work but knew that my successor, Shan
Cooper, the first African American woman to hold this position,
faced some tough challenges. The $65 billion F-22 Raptor program
was cut because of budget reasons, and production would cease in
2012, leaving Lockheed scrambling to accommodate 1,500 workers
at the nine-hundred-acre plant. I think everyone was hoping that
maintenance on the F-22 would continue, and that upgrades to the
C-5 Galaxy (the largest military transport aircraft) and the addition
of the F-35 would all be part of Marietta's future plans. I was proud
of what I had accomplished, but that future would have to proceed
without me.

CHAPTER 10
THREE CONVERSATIONS

*"Retirement feels like
stepping off a cliff."*

DECIDING TO RETIRE when you have been a CEO, executive, or high-level manager is a complex and emotional process, fraught with anxiety and uncertainty. I left Lockheed Martin Marietta in 2011 and am regularly asked by colleagues about how I made my decision to finally leave. These conversations are often filled with uncertainty and anxiety, but at the heart of each conversation is one question (though they rarely ask it outright): How can I stay relevant and remain respected? One of the biggest concerns they express is transitioning from being in charge to feeling insignificant. Retirement feels like stepping off a cliff, as one colleague said after being pushed out of his position: "I wake up five days a week with nothing to do."

There are dozens of articles written for executives contemplating retirement, and they offer solid advice for anyone facing this major life decision. Retiring CEOs almost all share the same dilemma. They are focused so much on building and running their companies that they give almost no thought to what it would look like when they hand the reins to their successor. *Harvard Business Review* published "The CEO's Guide to Retirement" in September 2018, and it is filled with solid advice. In it, the authors Marc A. Feigen and Ron Williams recount a range of anecdotes. Bill Weldon, former CEO of Johnson and Johnson explained, "I didn't do a lot of thinking about post-employment while I was still CEO. As a result, I went off the ramp at 110 miles an hour and quickly hit zero. Retirement was a black hole."

The average age of retirement for CEOs is sixty-two, and there are very few roadmaps to guide you for the next two or possibly three decades. The *Harvard Business Review* article mentioned above offers practical advice: Plan your off-ramp; take your time; prepare to deal with yourself; partner with your partner; assume the role of mentor; plan your allocation of time; and give back. These are all terrific suggestions, but they skirt what I see as the biggest issue: What are the psychological adjustments that you will need to make in this transition? While some people are excited to retire and are literally counting the days, I more often encounter high-level executives whose identities are so intertwined with their positions that it is hard to even consider leaving a company. They are where they work and giving up their identity is terrifying.

In an April 12, 2018, *Forbes* article, "Are You a (Former) Boss Who Just Won't Go Away?," Roger Dean Duncan addresses this issue: "In many cases, the reluctance to move on has nothing to do with finances. Some folks just can't imagine life without the job. Maybe their self-identity is too closely linked to title and position. Maybe they just cannot fathom doing something 'new.'" Duncan addresses another challenge, the retired executive who will not leave. He tells the story about working as an executive coach for a global technology firm. One day on the job, he saw a man in an elegant office reading the paper. When asked about it, he learned that the man "had no specific duties or responsibilities. He attended no meetings and interacted very little with anyone. But he came to the office every day and read the newspaper." And the firm was paying him $500,000 a year to be on retainer. A number of companies have executives who won't quit—evidenced by the high-profile case of Don Hewitt, the longtime producer of *Sixty Minutes*. He would not retire, and finally he was asked to step down and hand the reins to Jeff Fager in 2004. Even then, he stayed an advisor to Fager and executive producer for CBS. Employees like Hewitt pose a range of problems— from trying to micromanage their successor or becoming impediments to the company's growth. I was not going to be that person. After I left, I only reached back to my successor when I saw a pressing issue that needed her attention. At those rare times, I sent a brief email and gave her the opportunity to reach out to me if she needed background information or advice. That happened only a few times, mainly in the first year.

Many executives, especially those in high-profile positions, do not get to choose when to retire. They are often pushed out by public scandals, consolidations, or because they conflict with the boards of directors. Businesses often want executives to leave by the age of sixty-five to mitigate the expense of their high wages and increased drain on health care plans. In "Dealing with Aging Executives Who Just Won't Quit," published in the February 2, 2003, issue of the *New York Times*, Patrick McGeehan explains: "Top executives like these seem inclined to see themselves as tenured professors. . . . And university professors with tenure are among the best protected groups of professional employees: they are virtually guaranteed jobs for as long as they can do them." ProPublica reported on January 4, 2019, that workers over fifty, regardless of their rank or position, are often pushed out of long-term jobs. The article explained that "ProPublica and the Urban Institute, a Washington think tank, analyzed data from the Health and Retirement Study, or HRS, the premier source of quantitative information about aging in America. Since 1992, the study has followed a nationally representative sample of about 20,000 people from the time they turn 50 through the rest of their lives." They concluded that 56 percent of older workers are laid off and suffer damaging financial circumstances.

Hollywood has depicted retirement as a time filled with uncertainty, anxiety, and sometimes humor—which does not offer much comfort. The 2002 film *About Schmidt* features Jack Nicholson as a newly retired insurance actuary and recent widower. Without a wife or job, he decides to drive his Winnebago Adventurer motor home to visit his daughter, then places that had been important to his past, as he searches for meaning in his life. Other films—ranging from *The Lion in Winter* (1968), *On Golden Pond* (1981), *Grumpy Old Men* (1993), *Cocoon* (1985), *Lost in America* (1985), *Unforgiven*

(1992), *Calendar Girls* (2003), *The Bucket List* (2007), *The Best Exotic Marigold Hotel* (2011), and *Poms* (2019)—document the twilight of careers and lives with a kind of bemusement. But retirement is anything but entertaining.

My decision to retire was not sudden; it took nearly half a dozen years to reach the conclusion that it was time for me to step down. I had seen many of my colleagues—top-level managers—struggle to leave their prestigious and high-paying positions. I knew I wanted to avoid making the same mistake. But I also loved the work I was doing; Lockheed was thriving and growing, so I had no compelling reason to leave. There was no scandal or major downturn that was prompting my decision. The timetable was my own.

My decision to leave Lockheed was guided by three conversations: one with Coretta Scott King (the widow of Dr. Martin Luther King Jr.), a second with my longtime colleague Bob Stevens, and a third with my wife and two sons during a football game. This chapter will resonate with anyone who is struggling to make this transition.

The first conversation I had about retirement occurred at a Martin Luther King Jr. celebration in Atlanta in 2005 with Coretta Scott King, a year before she died. Each January, Lockheed joined other corporations and organizations in sponsoring an annual citywide celebration of Atlanta's favorite son. Carolyn Long Banks (the first black woman to serve on the Atlanta City Council) and Hamilton Holmes Jr. (son of Dr. Hamilton E. Holmes, who helped desegregate the University of Georgia) were both Lockheed employees and knew the King family well. They helped coordinate Lockheed's participation. At the VIP reception before the event, I found myself talking to Mrs. King. We knew each other but were not close personal friends. I expected to pay my respects, make some small talk, and then allow her to greet the other guests. I was not planning on having a heartfelt conversation about retirement. I knew she had been ill, so maybe that is what prompted her musing on the subject, but I remember her saying to me: "Lee, it's better to leave one year early than one year too late." Her brief comment at the end of our talk really resonated with me. My mother died in 1992 at the age of sixty-four, just six months shy of when she was scheduled to retire. My father died in 2001 at seventy-seven and never had a chance to stop working. By 2005, I had been at Lockheed for about five years, and that conversation with Mrs. King was the first time I thought about what my life might look like after leaving a full-time job.

The second conversation was equally unexpected. I was in Washington, D.C., at an ethics meeting for Lockheed in 2007, and during a break I found myself at the sink washing my hands in the restroom with Bob Stevens, who was then chairman of the board. He knew I had prostate surgery in 2006, and the conversation soon focused on my recovery. I talked for a few minutes about how it was going and noted that I was not bouncing back as quickly as I had before. I had never said that to anyone and really had never even thought about it. Bob had a way of putting people at ease and always had a genuine interest in the lives of his colleagues and friends. This was not a conversation between business colleagues but rather a genuine discussion between two men in their fifties contemplating retirement and facing their mortality. In 2007, I had been at Lockheed for seven years, and Bob and I had built a strong, trusting relationship after working on a number of complex projects. He turned out to be the first person I confided in that I was really feeling my age and starting to think about what life would look like after Lockheed.

My third conversation came on a Sunday evening in September 2009 at home while watching football with my family in Atlanta. Broderick was in town from Indianapolis for an annual leadership meeting that he, Evelyn, and Roderick attend in Atlanta each year; it had become a tradition in our family. The meeting ended on Sunday afternoon, and Broderick typically stayed the night to watch football with the family. I made ribs and wings on my Big Green Egg and spent hours in the kitchen experimenting with various sauces to serve as condiments. The Indianapolis Colts were playing, and when dinner was ready, we all gathered around the table for dinner. Not five minutes into the meal, Evelyn looked up and said, "It's good to have the family together. This is so rare for us these days, and I really miss it." I was scheduled to fly to Fort Worth the next day, and I could tell that my work and travel were having a negative impact on my family. I discovered that there were typically three kinds of executives—those who genuinely loved to travel and embraced it, those who used it to escape life's realities, and those who tolerated it. I knew travel was part of the game, but I was certainly getting tired of it. Without prompting, Roderick said, "Dad, we would love to have you around more. You have worked for so long, maybe it's time to take a break." Broderick nodded in agreement; they both saw that I was slowing down.

They were right. I had seen what overwork had done to many colleagues; rarely does someone leave the highest levels of corporate American entirely whole. They often have neglected their families and friends, have health issues, or have simply run out of steam. During my time at GM, Rolls-Royce, and Lockheed, I found myself at funerals for colleagues who were much younger than I was. The saddest part of those affairs was that, in some cases, the church or funeral home was nearly empty. My colleagues had spent more time at work and trying to maintain their power than on building relationships, and that was on full view at their funerals. Their families struggled to say good things about them.

That brief exchange during a commercial break during a Sunday night football game stopped me in my tracks. It was clear that the boys and Evelyn had been talking about retirement without me because they were not sure how to broach the subject. They had realized that I was slowing down and became concerned about my health. I was no longer the Energizer Bunny who could keep going and going. I made my decision that night to begin planning for my exit. My family was telling me that it was time to get out, and they were encouraging me to take control of the end of my career before it was too late. Taken together, these three conversations between 2005 and 2009 helped me solidify a plan for my next steps.

It would take me about eighteen months to finalize the process. I called Ralph Heath, executive vice president for Lockheed Martin Corporation and president of Lockheed Martin Aeronautics Company, and Chris Kubasik to tell them I was planning to leave and then started a round of phone calls to business, community, and political leaders who had been so supportive of my work at Lockheed.

After my formal announcement in January 2011, Bob Stevens invited me to come to Lockheed's headquarters in Bethesda, Maryland. After our meeting, we had a sandwich and a cup of coffee. Our conversation flowed freely and felt just like the ones I remembered having with my teenage friends at the shoeshine stand in Fort Pierce. We laughed, joked, and ribbed each other. He knew that I had been working all my life and that I was ready to walk away. I had a number of retirement celebrations, but these informal meals, including a crab dinner with Ralph, were my favorites.

On the evening of March 22, 2011, the Cobb Chamber of Commerce hosted an event to honor my work at Lockheed. It was a chance for me to reflect on my past eleven years at the plant, and I was surprised to see Ralph Heath, who had flown in from Fort Worth to attend. Ralph spoke at the event and said some very kind things about my work at Lockheed: "Lee has stood for everything we hold up in terms of our core values as a company at Lockheed Martin. His leadership, his business acumen, and frankly his credibility that he established with our customers at all levels and his leadership of our workforce has been impressive." Dr. Joseph Lowery, the well-respected minister and civil rights leader, also made some remarks. I recall him saying, "When Lee came to Lockheed, we thought he was an Uncle Tom, and that proved to be a lie. The rest of you thought he was a token hire, and that was a lie. What all of us are saying is accept our apologies for our first impressions and know how much we appreciate everything you have done for Lockheed, for Georgia, and for the African American community." At that event, the *Marietta Daily Journal* published an article that was written about me when I arrived and one about my retirement. The House of Representatives even got in on the act and passed House Resolution 638 in my honor, commending me for my "efficient, effective, unselfish, and dedicated service to the security of our nation."

My last day at Lockheed was May 1, 2011. My successor, Shan Cooper, was a terrific choice and became the first African American woman to assume this level of leadership at Lockheed. She is the daughter of a pastor from Anniston, Alabama. She had an MBA from Emory University and a master's degree in human resources from Rutgers. She joined Lockheed Martin in 2002 as part of a diversity management team and was later named vice president. She was graceful, smart, and compassionate but could be tough when needed. I brought her to Marietta because I learned early on that she was someone that you could trust. I sat in on the interviews to hire my replacement, and when Shan was named Lockheed Martin Aeronautics Company vice president and general manager, I was pleased to know that I was leaving the company in capable hands. She had been a great colleague and friend. Shan stayed in this position at Lockheed for five years, stepping down in February 2016 to join the executive team of WestRock, a Fortune 500 company co-headquartered in Richmond, Virginia, and Norcross, Georgia.

After leaving Lockheed, I wanted to spend a few months getting organized. For many years, I had tried to write a memoir, and I knew that retirement would give me time to devote to understanding how a sharecropper's son could end up in leadership at one of the nation's most respected companies. I had always been a voracious reader, and I was really looking forward to having time to catch up on all I had missed while working sixty to seventy hours per week. I used to joke to my friends that I was preparing to go on *Jeopardy!* Evelyn and I watched *Wheel of Fortune* and *Jeopardy!* every night, and it was for me a casual rehearsal for the real thing. I tried out for the show but never received a call back. I had plenty of other things to occupy my time, notably my health.

I had endured several surgeries: on my gallbladder (in 1996), prostate (in 1980 and 2006), sinus (2000), and knee (2005). I was suffering from hypertension, a common condition in African American men of a certain age, and was gaining weight because my fitness program could not keep pace with my work schedule. Because my mother died early, I was worried about following in her footsteps. I was always convinced I would die in my sixties. I was also worried about Evelyn, who had completed her second treatment for uterine cancer in 2010. I saw so many friends and family become ill and infirm, so Evelyn and I focused all of our energy on reclaiming our health. We also wanted to spend more time traveling. She used to say that she wanted her high school boyfriend back—which was me—and was worried that if I did not slow down that I would not be in any condition to enjoy my retirement. After leaving Lockheed, we took trips to Paris, Israel, Rome, and London and truly relaxed, and I enjoyed the opportunity to explore those amazing places without worrying about work.

But what gave me the most joy in retirement was simply spending time in public places with regular people. I did not want to retire to a private country club; I had more fun hanging out at Starbucks and Target. After being an executive in a large corporation, I found that I had lost touch with a range of activities that most people do every day—stop for coffee, eat lunch at a restaurant, go to the grocery store. I recalled reading about President Dwight D. Eisenhower in his retirement in Gettysburg. He had largely been sequestered from the American people from the time he entered West Point until the end of his second term for president. He had never dialed a telephone; he had not driven a car and did not have a driver's license. Other places like dry cleaners, movie theaters, bowling alleys, and supermarkets were utter mysteries to him. After he retired, he used to go to the local grocery store and bring home food for Mamie to try, much to her consternation.

I felt much like former President Eisenhower and would dress casually on Fridays and go to Lassiter High School football games. During the week, I visited Barnes and Noble, Walmart, or Target and walked aimlessly down each aisle to see what was new. I talked with employees and fellow shoppers and befriended a woman in Target who worked in electronics. I would often find myself looking through the bargain bin at movies that I had missed seeing in the theater. We would see each other a few times a week, and I think she thought I might have been homeless. One day, when I walked in, I saw her in the restaurant at the front of the store. She called out to me to join her for lunch. She knew which days I came in and had saved half of her pizza for me. Here was this young woman making minimum wage worrying about me. I was truly humbled and touched by her generosity. A few years later, we encountered each other at an event, and she was stunned to learn that I had been a Lockheed executive.

What was notable about these adventures was how frustrated and anxious people were. Employees and fellow shoppers often talked about their jobs and bosses with frustration and were worried about their children's education, their families, and what the future held. The world had shifted. It was no longer possible to get a job at General Motors or a similar company and spend your whole career there, raising a family and planning for retirement. Good, well-paying jobs were scarce, and the gig economy (where companies hire independent workers for short-term commitments) made people feel unsettled. Though I was not officially doing research, these testimonials showed me how most people really lived.

Retirement also gave me a chance to slow down and decide how I wanted to continue to serve my community. I determined that education would be my main focus. I agreed to serve on the advisory board for the Coles College of Business at Kennesaw State University, which was only about ten miles from my home. I was named an executive-in-residence and regularly met with Dean Kathy Schwaig, students, and faculty. This work with KSU afforded me some structure and helped me keep up with the research and trends that were shaping the business world. In 2016, I was honored to be included in the second class of the Coles College of Business Hall of Fame along with Jack Dinos. Established in 2015, the Hall of Fame recognizes Coles College's most esteemed supporters. I also served as a trustee of my alma mater Bethune-Cookman from 2000 to 2012. In 2010, the university opened the Lee Rhyant Residential Hall to honor my service. Evelyn and I also created the Lee and Evelyn Rhyant Foundation, which supported local nonprofits.

What was especially satisfying about this work was the chance to see exemplary female leaders in action. I left Lockheed in the capable hands of Shan Cooper, and in my retirement, I worked closely with Dr. Kathy Schwaig at KSU and mentored young executives. It was heartening to see how much the world had changed and how common it was to see women in positions of power. In 1972, when I started at General Motors, the executive ranks were dominated by men. Today, women leaders are making their mark and reshaping entire industries. *Harvard Business Review* reported in 2012 that women are more effective leaders in a number of core competencies, from taking the initiative and developing others to inspiring and motivating teams and pursuing their own development. I saw that firsthand.

Any big life change makes you more reflective, and retirement was no different. I do not want to suggest that my transition was seamless; it was much more nuanced than these three conversations reveal. One event that happened a year before I retired made that abundantly clear. I had come a long way from Sasser, Georgia. One day when Evelyn was in Florida, I found myself back in my hometown. I had gotten up on the morning of Saturday, June 12, 2010, and threw on an old pair of shorts and a T-shirt and flip-flops and headed to the QuikTrip to grab a cup of coffee. The next thing I knew, I was in Sasser, the town in which I was born—five hours away. I have almost no memory of making that drive. I had not planned to go, but something pulled me south. I had been working on my memoir and was being nagged by a question: How did I get out of this one-horse town? It was a sad place—poor and dying. It looked nothing like the small town "loaded with antiquing fun" as advertised on exploregeorgia.org. Sasser had 304 residents, 26 percent of whom live below the poverty rate.

I got out of my car and stood in downtown wondering: Why is my life so different from the kids who grew up here? What would have happened if I had stayed? You could just feel the misery of this town—except for a few antique stores, it was empty and felt a lot like the way my mother and father had described it to me as a child. I stayed for about an hour before heading back. I was driving my Cadillac, and a few miles outside of town, I was pulled over by a white Terrell County police officer. After seeing how I was dressed, I am sure he ran the license plate on my car to see if it was stolen. He left me sitting in the Cadillac with his lights flashing for about half an hour—likely confused by the situation. Hell, I was confused by the situation. He finally came back to the car, mumbled something about my taillight, and let me go without a ticket. I stopped at the first Walmart I saw to buy some clothes to change into and sped like hell back to Atlanta.

CHAPTER 11
ANY TWO FOOLS CAN FIGHT

*"That's just politics. After
six o'clock, we're buddies—
we're friends."*

I RECENTLY CAME ACROSS an archived article from *Forbes* from
2012 that opened with a few sentences that stopped me in my
tracks. Mike Myatt, the magazine's leadership columnist and
founder and chairman of N2Growth, wrote in "Five Keys of Dealing
with Workplace Conflict," "Here's the thing—leadership and conflict
go hand-in-hand. Leadership is a full-contact sport, and if you cannot or will not address conflict in a healthy, productive fashion, you
should not be in a leadership role." Reflecting back on my career, I
realize now that, while it may have taken me a while to reach the
same conclusion, Myatt was right. How you approach and manage
conflict will shape the trajectory of your career, and it can often be
the difference between success and failure.

While working on a union contract at General Motors, I came to
know a United Auto Workers (UAW) negotiator named Bill Shoemaker who fundamentally changed the way I approached conflict.
Bill was chief negotiator for the UAW, and we were tangled in a complex contract negotiation after Rolls-Royce purchased Allison Engine and just before I left the company. Founded in 1935 under the
umbrella of the American Federation of Labor (AFL) in Detroit, the
UAW was a powerful and active union that pushed the auto industry to improve the working conditions and wages for their workers.
I was part of the management team at Allison, and Bill was leading

the union effort. We were in the last days of a three-month contract negotiation, and all of the local issues had been resolved. That left the national issues on the table that would affect every UAW member, and the major sticking point was benefits. I do not remember all of the details, but it was contentious.

Management and labor are natural adversaries, and the process had been grueling. Bill did not take an active role in the meetings until the last several days. He was a stately, older man who was always well dressed and displayed genteel manners. If you imagine a union boss to be a salty, cursing bully who might have been as comfortable in a boxing ring as on a factory floor, that was not Bill. He was as much a gentleman in his dealings with the union rank and file as he was with the management. In the last days of the negotiations, he spent most of his time with Mike Hudson, our top management official in Indianapolis. I found myself in a series of increasingly heated meetings that were starting to get out of control—there were verbal assaults and elevated emotions. It was exhausting, and during a break, I ran into Bill in the hallway. He could see that my frustration was mounting. While I was getting a drink of water, he came over to chat. It was mostly small talk, but I do remember that before he left, he leaned over to me, smiled, and whispered: "Any two fools can fight. That's the easy part. The real work is in coming up with a resolution that everyone can accept." I thought back to my time at GM with Tom and the scrap tickets. When Bill joined the meetings in the final two days, the whole dynamic in the room changed. He took the temperature of the room, and with a kind of quiet confidence, he took immediate control of the situation to get the negotiations back on track. He was firm but reasonable and gave everyone assurance that the solution was within our grasp. He helped us settle the contract and, not long after, retired.

What he said to me at the water fountain really got me thinking. In that situation, I was in management and had a fair amount of responsibility in negotiating the new contract. I wanted to prove myself worthy but was becoming frustrated with the lack of progress and was starting to feel my patience wane and my temper rise. It would have been easy to blow up, scream and shout, and posture like a peacock, just as the other people around the table started to do. But Bill helped me step back and rethink my approach. We were not likely to end up with a win-win situation, where everyone was happy about everything. All negotiations require compromise. But after my conversation with Bill, I came to believe that we had to change our approach and better manage our expectations.

I came into future meetings with a new priority—to find common ground, to understand what was motivating the other side, to consider how they would have to message whatever deal we struck to their constituencies, and to put every option on the table that might lead to a more collaborative solution. Fighting, digging in, bullying, and becoming angry is the quickest way to lose compassion and abdicate responsibility for resolving anything. But I was not naive. I knew I was going to get a lot of push back afterward and hear: "You sold us out! You capitulated! You gave up too much!" That is exactly what happened, but I tried to counter by explaining the process, our goals, and why the compromise was the best option going forward. I experienced the most resistance from my own side, just as I suspected the other side did from the union members. It made me think about the line spoken by Albus Dumbledore, headmaster of Hogwarts, to Neville Longbottom in J. K. Rowling's book, *Harry Potter and the Sorcerer's Stone*: "There are all kinds of courage. It takes a great deal of bravery to stand up to our enemies, but just as much to stand up to our friends." I felt I had made a fair decision based on Bill's advice and started to change my approach to relationships with people that had the potential to become adversarial—union members, government contractors, and auditors. It also changed how I viewed my personal relationships, which was an added dividend.

Bill was not my only inspiration regarding conflict. I remembered reading as a young man about the friendship between Dr. Martin Luther King Jr. and President Lyndon B. Johnson. They were both leading in a tumultuous time and developed a personal relationship based on their mutual support for civil rights. Johnson often invited King to the White House to discuss possible avenues of cooperation, and the strength of their relationship led to the passage of the Voting Rights Act of 1965, which changed the course of American history. After King was shot on April 4, 1968, Johnson issued Presidential Proclamation 3839 designating Sunday, April 7, 1968, as the day of national mourning for his longtime friend.

Republican president Ronald Reagan (1981–1989) and Democratic Speaker of the House Tip O'Neill (1977–1987) also had a notable relationship, one that by every measure should have been driven by conflict. They could not have been more diametrically opposed to each other, but they never let their politics define their relationship or their service to their country. O'Neill once reflected on something disparaging about Reagan that was reported in a newspaper with, "That's just politics. After six o'clock, we're buddies—we're friends." I do not want to simplify a relationship that I knew nothing about personally, but it was significant that they often socialized together and maintained a warm friendship. Once in a meeting that was heated, Reagan set his watch to six o'clock to remind them of the nature of their friendship. Thomas O'Neill, the lieutenant governor of Massachusetts from 1975 to 1983 and son of Tip O'Neill, wrote in an October 5, 2012, article in the *New York Times* entitled "Frenemies: A Love Story" that the relationship between the two men, "should serve as a model for how political leaders can differ deeply on issues, and yet work together for the good of the country." He goes on to describe them as "two men who were from humble Irish-American backgrounds who did not back down from a fight, and their worldviews were poles apart." Thomas O'Neill recalled, "President Reagan knew my father treasured Boston College, so he was the centerpiece of a dinner at the Washington Hilton Hotel that raised $1 million to build the O'Neill Library there. When Reagan was shot at the same hotel, my father went to his hospital room to pray by his bed." They were not close friends, but after work, they shelved their differences, even if temporarily, and sat down for drinks at the White House. In today's political climate, I find that pretty amazing.

I was also inspired by a story told by Dr. Betty Siegel, the long-serving president of Kennesaw State University who died in February 2020. In speeches, she recounted a fable about conflict: "There is a story about a Native American, a Cherokee, teaching his grandson about life. 'A fight is going on inside me,' he said to the boy, 'a terrible fight, between two wolves. One is evil. He is anger, sorrow, regret, greed, arrogance, self-pity, guilt, resentment, lies, false pride, superiority, and ego. The other is good. He is joy, peace, love, hope, serenity, humility, kindness, benevolence, empathy, generosity, truth, compassion, and faith. The same fight is going on inside of you and inside of every other person.' The grandson thought about it for a long moment, and then he asked his grandfather, 'Which wolf will win?' The old Cherokee grandfather simply replied, 'The one you feed.'"

Another source that gave me insight into conflict was Pulitzer Prize–winning author Doris Kearns Goodwin's 2005 book *Team of Rivals: The Political Genius of Abraham Lincoln.* I bought a copy of the book when I learned that President Barack Obama was inspired by it when creating his own cabinet. Focused on Lincoln from 1861 to 1865, Goodwin explains how the new president used conflict to his advantage. Three of his cabinet members—Attorney General Edward Bates, Secretary of the Treasury Salmon P. Chase, and Secretary of State William H. Seward—were all men who had run against Lincoln in 1860. Lincoln actively sought out his adversaries and brought them together to create probably the most politically diverse cabinet in history. He managed their personalities, marshalled their talents, listened to their unvarnished advice, and ultimately won their respect and admiration. By actively seeking dissenting voices, Lincoln created an environment that was rife with conflict but also filled with honesty and commitment to a cause. It is an extraordinary story about an inexperienced president and an adversarial cabinet, but it is a powerful lesson on leadership and managing conflict. In explaining his choices, Lincoln said, "We need the strongest men of the party in the cabinet. These were the very strongest men. Then I had no right to deprive the country of their services." That sentiment influenced how I hired and built my leadership team. I did not need to hire people who looked just like me, trained like me, or thought like me. I needed to hire a visionary and diverse team who had expertise and courage to tell me no. Leader-

ship teams composed of a single generation, race, or gender are rec-
ipes for disaster.

The advice of Bill Shoemaker, the examples of Martin Luther King
Jr. and Lyndon Johnson and of Ronald Reagan and Tip O'Neill, the
parable told by Betty Siegel, and the experiment of Abraham Lincoln all shaped me. I remember that I had a union member working for me named Virgil who was a constant source of frustration.
He worked the afternoon shift at GM where I was a supervisor and
he came in each day angling for a fight. After a few weeks of this, I
sat him down and said, "Virgil, we can keep on fighting like cats and
dogs, but I got to tell you I am sick of it. Let's try something different. For thirty minutes a day, you and I are going to sit down and
try to get along." So that's what we did. We set aside time every day,
and I came to understand what was really motivating him; his fellow workers wanted to see someone who was fighting for them every day. He did not want them to think he had given up or given in
to management, so he thought he needed to maintain an aggressive
posture for everyone to see. In the daily meetings, he confided in me
about his challenges and talked about what issues were important
to his constituents and what I could easily get fixed—from cleaning up the bathrooms to getting the water fountains repaired. After about three weeks of these conversations, we both started to see
each other's perspective. I tried to make sure he got the credit for the
changes. I discovered that while the other union members wanted a
fierce advocate, they were also tired of all the anger and bitterness.
We all ended up in a better place, and I think we both learned that
behind-the-scenes legwork and real compromise went a long way.
There was never a sense that either side had capitulated. Instead, it
looked as if we were just channeling Elvis Presley and were "taking
care of business."

I also discovered that my approach to conflict could help pave the
way for people to do the right thing. I remember a fellow manager
came to me explaining that he wanted to attend his coworker's father's funeral. He was white and his coworker was black, and it was
the 1980s and a tumultuous time in our country's racial history. He

was nervous about going to the funeral alone but really wanted to support his friend. I understood exactly what he was up against and told him I would take a vacation day to go with him. I knew the family of the man who died, so I called them to let them know that the manager was coming and that he felt uncomfortable and did not want to be a distraction. I felt I needed to reach out to help stave off what might have been a complicated situation. I could have just approved his day off and let him navigate a black funeral alone, but he needed the help, and I was in a unique position to make his situation a little bit easier.

I discovered through my work at General Motors and Lockheed that the greatest asset was people, but they could also be a company's greatest liability. Tanya Menon and Leigh Thompson, writing for *Harvard Business Review*, published an article entitled "Putting a Price on People Problems at Work" on August 23, 2016. I retired from Lockheed in 2011, but their article put into words much of what I witnessed in my career. They argue that managers waste more time and money on a cluster of intractable issues, interpersonal conflict, miscommunication, poor decision-making, hiring mistakes, and poor training. In a survey of eighty executives, they asked them to estimate the daily cost of twenty issues, and they "estimated wasting an average of $7,227.07 per line item per day, for a total of $144,542.30." At least half of the issues focused on conflict— from ignoring problems at work, self-censoring to avoid voicing relevant concerns, to unproductive conflict. The authors went on to evaluate how solutions often devolve into "spending traps" where they set aside money, time, energy, and other resources to solve problems instead of investing in leading, managing, and executing.

Managing conflict is another story, and there are hundreds of theories about what is an effective strategy. I found that the best approach usually required that I move through three stages. The first step was to gather information by listening to employees and studying the company's culture. This was especially important when I made the move to Lockheed and faced a number of complex issues, from labor inefficiency to racial tension. The second step was to identify the issues at hand. I found that a small problem could sometimes masquerade as a big problem if there were enough employees that were fanning the flames. Sometimes bigger problems—such as different values, lack of sensitivity to race or gender, or limited re- sources—manifested as a lot of little problems that were difficult to manage. It was almost like that Whac-A-Mole game at the fair. One problem would pop up and garner your attention, and then a sec- ond or third would distract you from the first. The third step was to identify the stakeholders, put them in a room together, talk honestly, and begin to work on a collaborative solution. The solution—while never perfect or wholly satisfactory for everyone involved—had to work both for the company and for those who had to execute it. A solution that only served the bottom line was never going to be fully embraced by employees. Something that helped employees and did not help the company would never see any real investment.

There are plenty of models to understand conflict. The Thomas- Kilmann Conflict Mode Instrument (TKI) holds that there are five key styles for managing conflict, which influenced my own ap- proach. Developed as a research tool in the 1970s by Kenneth W. Thomas and Ralph H. Kilmann, it has been used in business to measure conflict-handling behavior. The first four styles identi- fied in the TKI—forcing, accommodating, avoiding, and compro- mising—have their limitations. Forcing satisfies your concerns but not others'; accommodating results in a one-sided victory; avoiding never moves the ball forward; and compromising leaves both par- ties unsatisfied. The best model is collaborating, or cooperating, be- cause it seeks mutually satisfying solutions for everyone involved. This is not the quickest approach, but it is often the longest lasting.

I also discovered something else important in my career. Not everyone wants to resolve conflict. From my early days at General Motors, I read a lot of management journals believing that conflict is something that people try to avoid. Instead, I learned that there are actually "high-conflict people" (HCP) who thrive on discord and dissent. A November 21, 2017, article in *Psychology Today* explains that there is a personality type that demonstrates a "pattern of all- or-nothing thinking, unmanaged emotions, extreme behavior or threats, and a preoccupation with blaming others. They have a Target of Blame, whom they regularly bully, harass, blame, humiliate, annoy, spread rumors about, and subject to many other adversarial behaviors." I have encountered a number of HCPs in my career and found that they share a desire to be in constant turmoil and seem to use drama to distract from focusing on their own lives and their own work. This was an especially difficult personality type to deal with in negotiations because they never wanted to move the ball forward. They seemed to use drama and conflict to exaggerate their own importance and keep everyone else on edge.

The focus on high conflict people brings me back to my childhood standing on the corner in Fort Pierce, Florida, at the shoeshine stand. We were all teenage boys trying to find our way in the world, and I remember how many times we got into fights—either with each other, with teenagers from rival schools, or with members of our community. But even then, I always wondered, "Why are we fighting? What did we really win? Why bother with all this nonsense?" My demanding schedule in high school and my mentors pulled me away from the shoeshine stand. On the occasions when I would find my way back there, I was always struck by how little it had changed. Same corner, same stand, same fights. But I was not the same. I was forging a future for myself and saw the emotional toll that stagnation and hopelessness were taking on my friends who did not have the same opportunities that I enjoyed. My parents, my teachers, and my church all kept me from drifting aimlessly. When I strayed, I was snatched back onto that path by my parents, Mr. Hines, Mr. Little, and others. I had childhood friends who became defined by conflict. They needed conflict; it fueled them and gave them a sense of identity and importance. As adults, I saw many of these same men go home and take out their frustrations on their wives and children, often demeaning them and trying to keep them under control. They either resorted to physical violence or emotional abuse, and that has had a long-lasting impact on our communities. I see this even today.

In January 2020, I was at a funeral for Evelyn's sister Louise in Fort Pierce, Florida. She and I had become close over the years, and the family asked me to speak at her memorial service. I debated for a long time about what to say and decided to focus on how we developed such a tight bond, harkening back to my mother. When I was newly married and visiting my mother, she and I talked in the kitchen while she cooked sausages for breakfast. The conversation was moving along when she suddenly started lecturing me by saying, "I'm noticing that you are doing some things that are not making me proud. You have to promise me three things. You will let Evelyn finish her education and have a career independent from you. There may come a day when she needs to walk away from you, and if that happens, she needs to be able to support herself. You should never keep her from her family. You may not understand all of this now, but they are important to her, and you need to make it possible for her to maintain those close relationships. You also have to make sure her family is always welcome in your home." I heeded her advice and became very close to Evelyn's family, and I am a better man for it.

After the service, I had more than a dozen women come to thank me for my remarks. Many of them told me a version of the same story: They married young and their husbands would not let them finish their degrees or get jobs. Their husbands also isolated them from their families as a form of control. When their husbands died or they divorced, the women were often left without the tools to survive. They had never balanced a checkbook, had not held a job, nor were able to support themselves. One woman told me about taking a job at Walmart in her seventies because her husband had done nothing to provide for her after his death, despite her having kept house for him and raised his children. This was not just my generation. One man told the story about his daughter, who excelled at the Naval Academy in Annapolis then married a man who did not want her to work. Within fifteen years, he divorced her, and she was left without anything. I think that was what my mother was warning me against, and it was sound advice. I am glad I was smart enough to take it to heart.

Feeling powerless is one reason for conflict, but I discovered another reason was to garner attention, even if it was overwhelmingly negative. I sat on a community board that served underprivileged youth in Indianapolis, and each year we held a social event that helped raise funds. The committee was populated with community leaders, including a man whose sole purpose seemed to be to stoke dissent and controversy. Every time we solved one problem, he created another. He was disruptive and constantly critical. Nothing that anyone could do would make him cooperate, and it was exhausting. Walking to my car after one particularly frustrating meeting, I realized he had parked right next to me. As he approached the parking lot, I decided to ask some blunt questions: "What the hell is your problem? Why are you so difficult?" I was not sure what he was going to say, but surprisingly, he gave me a pretty honest answer. "I just like stirring the pot. I think it's fun to throw a wrench into everything and watch everyone squirm. You get the wrong person on a committee like me, and you'll never get anything done." I finally asked, "What do you get out of it?" And he smiled slyly and said, "Attention. All the attention. Everybody caters to me, and I don't have to do any work. If it doesn't work, I just quit and move on to the next thing." Two weeks later, he quit the committee, and we had a great event. But I never forgot that conversation. It helped me understand that the only way to engage with people like that was to get off their train. Do not let them drive. Some people cannot stand cooperation; they have lived with conflict for so long that they think if it ends, so will their status and power. That was certainly the case for this guy.

I also discovered something else about what fuels conflict—it is sometimes born of jealousy. After moving to Indianapolis and taking a job with General Motors, Evelyn, the boys, and I would come home at least once a year to see the whole family. I found that my old friends and even some of my family members were not too glad to see us. They did not much care about what I was doing or want to hear about our new life. I learned long ago that envy and jealousy are two different emotions. You can envy someone the ability to jump high or cook, but you are not jealous of them. You are envious because you lack what they have. Jealousy is a different animal, created by the sense that you are about to lose something. I think that my success—at GM or Lockheed—somehow caused them to reflect negatively on their own lives, that they lost some sense of dignity by recognizing that I had done well. It was an odd feeling, but it definitely shaped my relationships with friends and family back home.

All of the lessons I learned about conflict were hard won. I did not just wake up one morning and experience a revelation, though that would have been nice. My perspective on conflict took years to cultivate, but I found that being reflective about why people clash helped me reclaim my equilibrium and conserve my energy. Several years ago, I came across a quote by Ronald Reagan that summed up my perspective: "Peace is not the absence of conflict. It is the ability to handle conflict by peaceful means." Manage conflict, understand what motivates your colleagues, family, and friends, and do not let anyone drag you onto their train. You have the power to decide when to get on and off; use it judiciously.

CHAPTER 12
COMMON GROUND

*"Don't tell a damn soul
what I have told you."*

MY DESIRE TO FIND common ground and manage conflict shaped my career and guided me after I left Lockheed in 2011. A year after I retired, in 2012, I decided to start LER Solutions, a consulting company to advise chief executives and senior leaders on the challenges specific to executive leadership. I discovered in my executive positions at Allison and Lockheed that CEOs want to talk with other CEOs about strategic advice without being criticized or judged. I felt that I could be a helpful sounding board that was part psychologist, part career coach, and part best friend. I would often hear from clients, "Don't tell a damn soul what I have told you. I just needed to get that off my chest and talk through it with someone who is not at my company and who can give me unbiased advice without my looking stupid, indecisive, or weak." My clients often called and asked me to lunch or to have a drink, and after the requisite small talk, would launch into a very personal conversation about challenges they faced or their company or impending retirements. This baby boomer generation, born between 1946 and 1964, composed one component of my business.

But I also found myself advising a new group of leaders, not those at the end of the careers but those who had been working between ten and twenty years and were on the cusp of taking major leadership roles. This included Generation X (those born between 1965 and 1980) and millennials (those born between 1981 and 1996). Even though I primarily marketed my consulting company to senior leadership, a number of younger colleagues were calling me for advice. And these two groups are facing completely different challenges, often based on the years of their birth.

Generation X, known as the "middle child generation," is an understudied and often unappreciated group, but it has had a powerful influence on American culture. Sometimes called slackers or latchkey kids, Generation Xers are often eclipsed by baby boomers and millennials. Defined by popular culture, this generation was deeply influenced by MTV and films like *Ferris Bueller's Day Off*. But as *Forbes* magazine declared in its September 13, 2016, article "The Undetected Influence of Generation X," they are highly educated (35 percent have college degrees, compared to 19 percent of millennials). They are often responsible for startups and new innovations—think Elon Musk and Jeff Bezos. They saw the first Apple Macintosh computer sold in 1984 and witnessed the crash of 1987 and the fall of the Berlin Wall. My two boys, Broderick and Roderick, fall into this generation, and while they face a number of challenges, it is women in this group whose lives are especially complex.

Generation X is sometimes called the "sandwich generation" because members are caught between raising children and caring for their elderly parents. Many Gen X women had children later in life, and medical advances have helped their parents live longer, often managing complicated chronic health conditions. Generation Xers find themselves constantly being pulled between their Generation Z children and boomer parents, and the burden most often falls on women. In January 2020, the *Atlantic* published an article entitled "Gen-X Women Are Caught in a Generational Tug of War." Journalist Ada Calhoun interviewed Amy Goyer, AARP's national family and caregiving expert and the author of *Juggling Life, Work, and Caregiving*, who explained the challenge: "More women are working. When you're trying to work while juggling caregiving and trying to have a life and maintain your primary relationship, it really affects you." A recent Pew Research study found that 48 percent of members of Generation X provide primary care for their aging parents, and 34 percent say their parents rely on them for emotional support.

Generation Xers share a focus on financial anxiety. They often have more debt than their parents, often from student loans and credit cards. In 2016, PricewaterhouseCoopers conducted an employee financial wellness survey that found that 50 percent of Generation Xers expect to have to delay retirement, and 25 percent have trouble meeting monthly expenses. That should come as no surprise as they are having to foot the bill for raising children and caring for parents all while managing to pay off debt.

Millennials face another set of challenges; many began their careers in boom times and experienced their first major setbacks during the 2008 recession. Some lost their jobs and their homes and were facing the prospect of never having stable work again. As the economy started to improve, they confronted a new reality, where jobs are being automated and the gig economy made full-time, benefitted positions difficult to find. Like Generation Xers, they often have significant student loans and worry about making ends meet. Many millennials use credit cards to pay for monthly expenses and then struggle to make minimum monthly payments. I know a number of professionals with advanced degrees from top-tier universities in this age group who drive Lyft or Uber on the side just to survive each month. In August 2018, in an article by T. J. McCue, the news magazine *Forbes* estimated that nearly 57 million Americans participate in the gig economy, and by 2023, that will reach 52 percent of the workforce. Millennials dominate that market and find that the highest paying jobs for independent workers are in AI (artificial intelligence) and blockchain (data that is managed by computers and not owned by a single entity).

Although working in the gig economy has definite benefits—flexibility, variety, creativity, autonomy, and sometimes higher pay— there are notable downsides. Gig jobs do not offer stable salaries or traditional benefits like health care, sick leave, technology or office support, or retirement matching. Freelancers have to keep meticulous records and pay quarterly taxes. They often report higher levels of isolation and stress and are worried about where their next job will come from. Gone are the days where you graduated high school or college, joined a large company, moved up through the ranks, retired, and earned a pension. That was my experience with both General Motors and Lockheed. But so much has changed, and I found myself using the lessons I learned during my long career to help them navigate these new, unchartered waters.

On February 20, 2019, the *New Republic* published a fascinating article entitled, "The Missing Black Millennial." Describing this generation, author Reniqua Allen wrote: "As a generation, millennials are used to being misunderstood. Perhaps no generation has been so gleefully maligned in the press, which has produced a zillion think pieces casting millennials as entitled, lazy, mayonnaise-hating, over-educated pampered whiners who, in their blinkered narcissism, are selling out the human race. That caricature has slowly given way to a more nuanced picture of a generation profoundly shaped by the events of its time—9/11, the Iraq War, the Great Recession, climate change—and baleful socioeconomic trends: growing income inequality, staggering levels of student debt, stagnant wages. And yet, for all this new understanding, there remains a huge blind spot when it comes to black millennials in particular."

In my consulting, I was seeing a unique set of challenges among African American workers who witnessed Generation X colleagues, often their parents, benefit from affirmative action in earlier decades only to see those same commitments fall away for them. When these workers—14 percent of the millennial population are African American—are hired today, they are being offered smaller compensation packages, undesirable schedules, little administrative support, shared offices, and positions that do not confer the status or influence that they had come to expect. They also were witnessing a resurgence in racism and white supremacy—from the failed response to Hurricane Katrina in 2005 to the Unite the Right march in Charlottesville, Virginia, in August 2017. They came of age hoping that much of the racism of the past was behind them—that the playing field had been leveled, that they now lived in a postracial society. They never experienced Jim Crow. They studied the civil rights movement in school. They celebrated the first African American president of the United States—what could be more significant than that? They were supposed to inherit a world that had been made better by the boomers and Generation X, only to find the same book with a different cover.

In the *New Republic*, Allen summed up the general frustration: "Black millennials are increasingly asked for their ID when voting. We are still disproportionately being sucked into the criminal justice system. We have less access to health care and are likely to die at a younger age. We have to dress a certain way, so we aren't stopped by police at night. We are mocked for the way we look and disparaged for being angry and loud. Our sexuality, always expressed as something animalistic and promiscuous, is often still the subject of public indignation. Even the wealthiest, most successful black millennials can't protest peacefully without being called ungrateful and unpatriotic." My clients expressed many of these concerns, which further heightened their anxiety.

Add financial worry to the mix, and you will see that millennial men and women are struggling to survive in an anxious time. Many have teenage children who will soon leave for college, piling on to their financial burden of hefty mortgages and their own student loans. They find themselves financially strapped and anxious. My time talking to people in Walmart, Starbucks, and Target after my retirement gave me a unique perspective on these issues and helped me be a better consultant. But I saw one other challenge that united both Generation X and millennials—the powerful influence of technology. Both groups share a comfort and ease with technology that we boomers will never enjoy. They are smarter, faster, and use data in ways that we could never even have fathomed. I try to imagine how my work in the aeronautic industry with General Motors and Lockheed would have been different with the technology available to us today. But there are notable downsides, including the corrosive power of social media. When I was growing up, you could do something stupid or rude, and maybe ten people would know about it before it faded away. Today, if that happens, you find yourself on CNN with a million negative comments on Twitter that will last forever. In an instant, your reputation can be destroyed and your career prospects ruined.

In December 2019, a new threat emerged, one that has turned the world upside down. The World Health Organization (WHO) reported a mysterious illness with acute respiratory symptoms in Wuhan, China, the capital city of the Hubei province. With more than 11 million people, it is the ninth most populous city in China. On February 11, the WHO announced that this new version of the coronavirus would be called COVID-19. A month later, the virus was classified as a pandemic, which meant that "multiple countries are seeing sustained transmission between people of an outbreak causing disease or death." I cannot remember a time in my life when something like this has affected everyone on earth—not 9/11; not AIDS, Ebola, or Zika; and not the various flu pandemics of the twentieth century. This has been unprecedented, and it has affected the generations with whom I consult in varying ways.

The baby boomers are concerned about susceptibility to the virus because of advanced age and about the need for stability in retirement. Generation X is forced to balance caring for elderly parents who are at higher risk and attending to children who are out of school. As many move into their fifties and sixties, they are also facing the risk of forced early retirement because of layoffs or ageism. Millennials are concerned about the collapse of sectors of the gig economy that have helped sustain them. What all three groups share is an overwhelming sense of anxiety and even panic as the world starts to grapple with the reality of this disease. The pandemic has dramatically affected the global economy, crushing the travel, commercial aerospace, insurance, and auto industries. Supply chains have been disrupted, and business leaders are facing production, transportation, and logistical challenges. The situation evolves by the day, and by August 2021, the Johns Hopkins Coronavirus Resource Center noted 211,606,303 cases globally and 4,428,562 deaths. Those numbers just keep rising.

COVID-19 has been humbling. The elderly, people of color, and those with limited access to reliable health care seem to be disproportionately affected. I have heard from a number of my business colleagues as they try to grapple with this new reality—that no amount of technology or wealth can fully protect their companies or their workers. For me, I knew we were in trouble when I saw a story in *Forbes* on March 31, 2020, about Waffle House. As a Georgian, Waffle House holds a special place in my heart. Founded by neighbors Joe Rogers Sr. and Tom Forkner in 1955 in Avondale Estates, a suburb of Atlanta, Waffle House restaurants became popular, and yellow and black signs soon dotted the American landscape. It is always open and can survive nearly any disaster—from floods to hurricanes to tornadoes. The Federal Emergency Management Agency (FEMA) actually has something called the Waffle House Index to measure the severity of natural disasters. The speed by which the twenty-four-hour restaurant can get back into operation is one way that FEMA measures the impact on any given community and how much federal assistance is needed. The index resembles a stoplight: green means you can order from the full menu, yellow means a limited menu, and red means the restaurant is closed. In March 2020, 20 percent of the locations (about 420) were closed, which was unprecedented in the company's history. The remaining stores have been trying to sustain themselves with take-out business but without much success. And that was just in the first month of the pandemic. This was a very bad sign of what was to come.

On March 19, 2020, *Politico* invited leaders from a range of industries to reflect on what to expect—and many of them were on the money. Deborah Tannen, professor of linguistics at Georgetown, predicted: "Instead of asking, 'Is there a reason to do this online?' we'll be asking, 'Is there any good reason to do this in person?'" Tom Nichols, a professor at the U.S. Naval War College, expected that it will force people back to "accepting that expertise matters." He also believed it will "return Americans to a new seriousness, or at least move them back toward the idea that government is a matter for serious people." Amy Sullivan, director of strategy at Vote Common Good, assumed that religious worship would change under quarantine, expecting that there will be less reliance on local congregations and that more individualized contemplative practices will gain in popularity. Sherry Turkle, a professor of the social studies of science and technology at MIT, believed the virus would help us use our devices to "rethink the kinds of community we can create through them." Other contributors predicted an explosion in telemedicine, electronic voting, a revival of parks and outdoor spaces, and the development of a stronger safety net for caring for the ill and infirm.

What was notable about the *Politico* article was an absence of any discussion about leadership in the private sector. What role will business leaders play in reshaping American life and the global economy? In the midst of this crisis, it is difficult to even begin to answer this question. But one thing I know for sure—we will not rebound by turning on each other. Either we "learn to live together as brothers or perish together as fools." The words of Martin Luther King Jr. have never resonated with such power and relevance as they do today. We must find common ground. The real question is: Who is equipped and courageous enough to take up this challenge?

As I speak to my colleagues in leadership positions, they are simply stunned by the steady diet of bad news that changes by the hour and are unsure about how to proceed. They have never seen this kind of vulnerability—either in the economy or in the populace on such a global scale. One thing that seems sure is that the coronavirus had changed everything. Over the past year, I have had conversations with senators, college administrators, business leaders, and CEOs who have lamented how unprepared we were and how close their industries and institutions are to collapsing. COVID has changed the way businesses run, the way people shop and interact with each other. It changed the way we view public health. It has prompted innovation and adaptation but also anxiety and uncertainty. That was something I knew a great deal about. For some of my colleagues, this was the first time they had experienced these issues in a professional setting. They were like the gifted student who sails through school and is finally faced with a real challenge only to realize that they do not have the skills to cope. Growing up black in America is to know vulnerability. You live it every day. Becoming disabled early in my career and having to learn to walk again taught me something about fragility. These cumulative experiences also teach you something about resilience. There is an arrogance in American life—that we are stronger, safer, and better than everyone else—but this virus has showed how unprotected we really are. This moment reminds me of the 1951 movie *The Day the Earth Stood Still*. The question, though, is are we like the human race depicted in the movie—destructive, stubborn, and unwilling to change—or will we reinvent ourselves? Will it change the way we view leadership at national, state, local, and corporate levels? We have to face these tough questions if we are going to succeed.

Since the pandemic started, the Center for Creative Leadership has released a series of articles and white papers, including one by Bill Pasmore, Cindy McCauley, Alice Cahill, Mike Smith, Chuck Ainsworth, and Chuck Palus entitled "Turning Crisis into Opportunity: Preparing Your Organization for a Transformed World." The authors' central point is that leaders have the opportunity to "ignite transformational change," and often crises are the best times to take bold action. COVID certainly changed everything for everyone, but it also allowed leaders to measure the strength of their organizational culture as they pivoted to meet the new reality. They argue, "It's time to talk about pushing your organization toward reinvention, not retreat, and how you can start creating the 'after.'" To do that, leaders should follow this recipe for success: articulate a bold, flexible vision; cultivate a culture of innovation; and lead change with empathy and integrity. The authors close by reminding readers that "hardship is part of the journey." I could not agree more. I learned more from the times I struggled than when I succeeded, and I cannot imagine what it would have been like to lead Lockheed during a pandemic—trying to operate an aircraft manufacturing plant in a safe way, discussing highly sensitive programs that shaped national security on Zoom, or supporting employees who were struggling to keep their families afloat. But I believe big challenges can lead to big opportunities, and I cannot wait to see how we come out on the other side of this.

CHAPTER 13
ELEVEN GUIDING PRINCIPLES

*"You have to fight to keep learning
and doing the right thing for your
business, family, and community."*

I F THERE IS ONE THING I have learned in my career and in my personal life, it is that critical thinking, questioning conventional wisdom, and challenging your assumptions are never wasted exercises. I learned that lesson at the age of seventeen during my senior year of high school in Fort Pierce. Teachers in Florida went on strike, and to help the students finish out their year, the African American seniors from Lincoln Park, the segregated high school, were moved to the predominantly white Dan McCarty High School. The principal hosted an assembly and invited Carol Strange and me, the two student council presidents, to join him on stage. As we approached each other, she reached out her hand to shake mine. The black and white students were both anxious to see if this experiment would work. This was 1968—a year that would be marked by assassinations, protests, and racial strife. I was not sure what I was expecting, but I was keenly aware of how many school districts faced violence when trying to desegregate. Carol could have ignored me, but she did not. She smiled and shook my hand, and her generous gesture made a big difference in my life. When my wife, Evelyn, and I drove down to have lunch with Carol fifty years later, in 2018, the power of that moment flooded over me.

I decided to write this book not because I thought I had an extraordinary story—just the opposite. In many ways, my life has been fairly typical. I had loving parents, was raised in a small town, benefitted from dedicated teachers and mentors, went to college, was hired by respected companies, and retired in time to enjoy my grandchildren and travel with my wife. A closer look, though, shows something else. My great-grandfather was enslaved, and I was born into poverty in south Georgia after World War II. I was the fourth of eight children raised by a family of sharecroppers struggling to survive the last decades of segregation. I have learned a lot in my journey from the Jim Crow South to the executive ranks at Detroit Diesel-Allison, Rolls-Royce Aerospace Division, and Lockheed Martin. I was given access to an education and employment that few of my friends or family members were afforded. I enjoyed success, but not without help and a lot of hard lessons along the way.

This book, *Soaring*, offers me a chance to give back by sharing eleven guiding principles that have helped in my business and my personal life. There are hundreds of books, seminars, magazines, and articles about business ethics on topics from hiring to social responsibility to product safety. Considering the ethical dimension of these issues really focuses on one central question: What moral principles should guide our practices and policies to help us do the right thing for our companies, our colleagues, our customers, and our communities? The eleven principles discussed in this chapter seek to answer that question, and I recount stories that illuminate their significance. I have often been inspired by this quote from Oprah Winfrey, "Real integrity is doing the right thing, knowing that nobody's going to know whether you did it or not."

GUIDING PRINCIPLE 1. *Your past does not define your present.* Our family had been sharecroppers since the end of the Civil War, working in the cotton fields in Alabama and Georgia. When I was four years old, my mother sold her wedding ring and moved our whole family to Fort Pierce, Florida. I had a pretty hardscrabble childhood, and my parents struggled most of their lives to give their children a chance at higher education. Poverty and systemic racism can permanently set the trajectory of a whole life, but mine was altered by dedicated parents, good mentors, excellent teachers, and strong social institutions. My parents deserve most of the credit. They had high, unwavering expectations that helped us all rise above our circumstances. After I retired, I had an encounter that reminded me again that your past does not define your present. I often volunteered to run to Target to shop for my wife, Evelyn. I loved to walk around the store and see what they had on sale. It was a new world for me because I was always working and never had time to shop or enjoy a casual afternoon wandering around. On this particular afternoon, I saw one of the associates that I had come to know in the café at the front, and she invited me to join her for lunch. She had come to know my schedule and saved half of her pizza for me. I was humbled that this young woman making minimum wage worried about me. I was not a retired Lockheed executive; I had left that world in my past. I was just an average Target customer who had befriended some of the associates. My present was focused on enjoying the generosity of a friend.

I recall a moment in 1987 when my son Broderick was a sophomore in high school that also illustrates this principle. We were playing a pretty rough game of basketball at our home in Indianapolis, and I was pushing him around the court and fouling him quite a bit while denying it. I used to coach my boys when they were young, but now I was their competitor. At one point, I knocked him down pretty hard when he was going for a layup. He brushed himself off, got back into the game, and for the next fifteen minutes he played with a force that I had never seen or experienced. I knew he was a better player than I was, certainly younger and faster. But he had been holding back, trying to be respectful of me as his father. But when I knocked him down, it changed something. He realized that the past did not have to shape how he played the game right now. I appreciated his respect, but I taught him to play hard and pushed him to do his best. Now he was ready to show me what he had, and this lesson was more precious than beating him on any given Sunday on the court.

GUIDING PRINCIPLE 2. *You are expendable and replaceable, so constantly update your skills on the job.* Prepare yourself for the emotional rollercoaster that will define your career. You are going to face challenges, and how you handle them is the key to success. In the fall of 1976, I was diagnosed with a rare disorder in which my body's immune system started to attack my nerves. I was told I would never walk again and faced a long road to recovery. I had been at Detroit Diesel-Allison, a division of General Motors, for less than four years, and now I was a young black man with a major handicap. What saved me and my job? In those four years, I cross-trained in different departments, built strong relationships with union members and fellow managers, developed a reputation as a hard worker who was fair, reliable, and dedicated, volunteered to take on new and difficult assignments, and cultivated relationships with senior colleagues who became strong mentors. Imagine that you have a bank account, and when you do any of the things listed above, you make deposits. I had made enough deposits to insulate myself even when injured. Even if you invent something, build a company from scratch, or make millions of dollars for stockholders, you are still expendable. One day, you are going to have to leave, and you rarely get to decide when.

Today, I often hear companies say, "Employees are our greatest asset." But a quick review of the business headlines show that most companies treat them as an expendable resource. My friend Ron Gill used to say, "People are more loyal to companies than companies are loyal to people." The only way to counter this reality is to wake up every day thinking about how to better serve your company, colleagues, and customers all while building your own value. I faced a similar experience nearly twenty years after I lost the ability to walk. In December 1993, Detroit Diesel-Allison was purchased by an investment firm for $310 million, ending Allison's sixty-four-year relationship with GM. I was surprised when several key members of the management team approached me to join the buyout and become a partial owner. Twenty managers were included, but I was the only African American among that group. I dedicated more than twenty-two years to this company and was proud to see that my sweat equity made me essential. If you had asked me in 1972 if I would ever leave General Motors—that we fondly called "Generous Motors"—I would have laughed. Now I was about to take one of the biggest risks of my career.

In the spring of 2000, before I began my position as executive vice president and general manager at Lockheed Martin in Marietta, Georgia, I had major nasal surgery. It was complicated and painful, but the recovery gave me a rare chance to pause and reflect on my career. I was fifty years old and had not had a vacation for more than a few days since I started working full time in 1972. I used the time off to take stock of what I had learned at Detroit Diesel-Allison and Rolls-Royce and to think about what kind of leader I wanted to be at Lockheed Martin. This was a chance not to update my skills per se but to reflect on mistakes and shortcomings that I needed to address to be successful in my new position. I realized that my failures were often due to pride and a desire to win, and my successes came when I treated people with dignity. My parents had been sharecroppers and janitors, and when I was a child I wanted to be a garbage truck driver. These are all essential jobs that help businesses operate efficiently and effectively, so I started thinking about inverting my new company's organizational chart. What would it look like if the janitorial and maintenance staffs were on the top and the managers and supervisors were on the bottom? How might we retool and retrain—not our skills but our perspectives—and think about genuine appreciation for all work and let go of pride, power, and dominance. I used my recovery to take a long, hard look in the mirror and thought that maybe I was expendable, but I would make sure that my employees would not be. It changed my whole perspective and helped me walk into Lockheed with a newfound confidence that was born not of arrogance but of respect. In 2009, I was named the National Management Association's Executive of the Year. During my acceptance speech, I showed a photograph of Billy, a janitor at Lock-heed that I saw every morning. My tribute to him shows the importance of an inverted organizational chart.

GUIDING PRINCIPLE 3: *Do not let anyone tell you where you belong.* Act like you belong there, and you will find the courage. When I was ten years old, my parents worked as janitors at a junior college, and one summer my brothers and I helped sod the grass. It was grueling work in the hot Florida sun, and we gave our parents the money we earned. Looking for water, one day I wandered into the college cafeteria. Covered in dirt, I helped myself to cool water and some donuts and sat down with the white students to enjoy my treat. I violated every Jim Crow law without even knowing it, and this went on all summer. I came to know the cafeteria ladies, never realizing that the white students were paying for my snacks. If my family had found out what I was doing, I would have been severely reprimanded, and they may have been fired or worse. But I never questioned that I was welcome, and I still believe to this day that I had a right to be there. Now, I was not naive enough to be defiant and brash. I knew all too well what happened to a young, black boy in the South, evidenced by the brutal killing of Emmett Till five years earlier in Mississippi. But I always believed I had the power to decide where I belonged. Years later, when I had reached the executive ranks at General Motors and was invited into the executive dining room, I took my place at the table without hesitation.

In 1965, my mother heard my high school choir sing "Climb Ev'ry Mountain" from the 1959 Rodgers and Hammerstein musical *The Sound of Music*. Every time I received an award or reached a notable milestone, she would sing the lyrics to the song softly into my ear as she hugged me. It was her way of telling me to not let anybody decide where I belonged or how I was going to get there. I had to take responsibility for that. Her last words to me before she died were, "Lee, climb every mountain." Every time I moved into an uncharted territory or felt that I did not belong, I would hum it to myself. I had no idea that a single song would become such a powerful reminder of the importance of defining my own path. Do not let anyone decide where you belong. That is your right and privilege.

GUIDING PRINCIPLE 4. *Do not hate the person but rather the hate inside that person.* I faced both overt and subtle examples of racism throughout my life and career and saw a lot of hatred. But it would be disingenuous to say that racism was the only form of hate I experienced—hate comes in all forms. In my first week at Detroit Diesel-Allison, I would occasionally answer the phone and hear someone yelling racial epithets. This was in the early 1970s as a major industry was trying to desegregate, and it was a difficult transition. I understood that and never took the calls personally. The most brutal expression of hate I witnessed came on July 8, 2003, when Douglas Williams, an employee at the Lockheed plant in Meridian, Mississippi, gunned down fellow workers after briefly attending a mandatory ethics and diversity class. I was the head of Lockheed Martin in Marietta at the time and flew immediately to Meridian to help the workers and community heal. I always remember a story that Martin Luther King Jr. told after he was stabbed by Izola Curry, a well-dressed African American woman who suffered from mental illness, on September 20, 1958 at Blumstein's Department Store in Harlem while signing copies of *Stride toward Freedom.* She plunged a letter opener in his chest, and he nearly died. Later King received a letter from a white high school student in White Plains, New York, who read in the newspaper that the stab wound was so dangerous that if he sneezed, he would have died. Her letter told him she was glad that he did not sneeze. You might expect that those two women could have switched places, and it would have made more sense, but I found that hating the person was always a futile exercise. Then you become mired in anger and resentment. You have to be part of the conversation that helps change things. King was right, "Hate is too big of a burden to bear."

My mother helped me understand this principle probably better than anyone by encouraging me to challenge my assumptions. I remember as a teenager watching the moon landing with her on a small black-and-white television during my summer break from college. On July 20, 1969, Apollo 11 became the first manned mission to land on the moon. Neil Armstrong and Buzz Aldrin made history when they took the first steps on another planetary body. It was a thrilling moment that mesmerized the world. While most people remember the moon walk, my mother focused on the launch four days earlier, on July 16. While watching it, she turned to me to say, "You know, everybody has a different launch pad. They all start from a different place, and you have to understand that." At the time, it seemed like a casual mention in the midst of this historic moment, but I later understood what she meant. You have to meet people where they are, and when they are being difficult or intolerant, pause for a moment to understand what is motivating their behavior. Think about their launch pad. How were they raised and educated? What influenced them? Taking that time can help you in immeasurable ways, and I found her advice useful in multiple arenas, from union negotiations to family feuds.

GUIDING PRINCIPLE 5. *The most important part of your education happens outside the classroom.* I was fortunate to have attended a series of exceptional schools, including Lincoln Park Academy, Bethune-Cookman College, and Indiana University. But my work at H. D. King Power Plant in Fort Pierce, Florida, contributed more to my education than anything else. I started at the end of my sophomore year in high school and continued through my graduation from college in 1972. I began as a mechanics helper and found a small group of well-respected African American men who took me under their wing. They taught me about professional decorum and arranged informal apprenticeships within the plant. I learned to operate every machine on the floor and came to understand the complexity of welding, grinding, and drill press operations. They introduced me to the plant manager and engineers from Western Electric, who all seemed willing to help me learn to overhaul generators and turbines and hone other skills. It was here that I learned to read blueprints and other highly technical skills, something that served me well at both General Motors and Lockheed. All of these men, black and white, insisted that I call them by their first names. They were all much older than I was, and there was an unwritten rule in the South that you never called an adult by his first name. This was especially true if you were black. But they insisted, and this small gesture made me feel like I belonged. I can never repay all that they taught me, and I have placed a great deal of value on informal education.

The power plant was the gift that kept on giving. In 1986, I was the gear plant manager for Detroit Diesel-Allison, a subsidiary of General Motors, on a two-week trip to Germany and Switzerland touring machine manufacturers. Because of my teenage job at the plant, I knew how many of the machines were built, the theory behind their construction, and how to operate most of them. The European employees in these plants were amazed that I was the only person—not the engineers nor other specialists—who could figure them out. Because of my expertise, our team could make a reasoned decision about what to purchase. None of that knowledge came from a classroom.

My twin boys played a critical role in my emotional education. When they were about six, I came home from work one day and became angry with Broderick for leaving his clothes and toys all around the house. Roderick, who was always quick to defend his brother, asked for a family meeting. Evelyn, the boys, and I all sat down one afternoon, and Roderick took charge: "Dad, it's not fair for you to yell at Broderick, because you leave your stuff all over the house, too." He showed us a small piece of paper where he had recorded a dot every time in the last week that I left something out of place. He was right, and I apologized. But I was mad that he had called me out, and I went into the other room and punched a chest of drawers and fractured my hand. It was hard to be corrected by a six-year-old, but the moment taught me an important lesson about fairness. When the twins were older, I had to learn it again. I clearly had more work to do in this area. The three of us were playing basketball, and Roderick hit this amazingly lucky shot—freakishly lucky. To this day, I still do not know how he did it. I called a foul, and Broderick immediately came to Roderick's defense, "How can you not give Rod his two points when you have violated every single rule of basketball in the last hour? You have traveled, double dribbled, and shot from in front of where we agreed the foul line should be. When Rod finally gets his shot, you took it away from him." Again, he was right. I think I was aggravated by the way Rod strutted after making the shot. It really set me off. I gave Rod his two points and told them I was sorry. There was no chest of drawers to hit this time, so I said some precious words under my breath. All of these moments were critical components of my education, and they made it possible for me to try out new skills, learn from my mistakes, and reinvent myself. I have always respected the work of Crawford Loritts, a senior pastor at Fellowship Bible Church in Roswell, Georgia. Two of his quotes, in particular, resonate with me: "When you're born, you look like your parents. When you die, you look like your decisions." And secondly, "Emotions are great passengers but terrible drivers."

When I retired from Lockheed Martin, I began LER Solutions, a consulting company focused on helping professionals develop their executive leadership skills. I expected to work with CEOs and executive vice presidents, but I found that I was just as likely to attract midlevel managers. To understand the unique challenges of each generation, I read *Managing the Generation Mix: From Urgency to Opportunity* by Carolyn A. Martin and Bruce Tulgan. They ask one essential question: "How do you engage workers of all ages in sharing their time, talents, expertise, and experience so that collaboration, high morale, and productivity become the hallmarks of your team?" In the introduction, the authors invite readers to take a "Generational IQ Test," which includes ten questions, including: (1) "I respect authority and follow the rules—but that authority has to earn my respect by being ethical and fair. Otherwise, I will do all I can do to circumvent the rules." And (2) "I think working from home is a bad idea. Out of sight, out of mind." I was pretty confident that I would do well, then I took it and flunked. I think I answered only five questions correctly. Did I really know what motivated younger generations? I clearly still had a lot to learn.

I came of age during the 1960s and 1970s and am no stranger to protest. I witnessed flag burnings, antiwar demonstrations, and assassinations and saw the power of nonviolence so championed by Dr. Martin Luther King, John Lewis, and other civil rights leaders. I have also lived through several major wars and seen how each new generation defines and advocates for social justice. But I also realized that older generations often think younger ones are more revolutionary and less respectful than their own. The Martin and Tulgan book disabused me of that notion, but so did a series of conversations about widening my viewpoint. During the civil rights movement, the conflict was primarily defined as an issue between black and white. Today, the fight for social justice spans LGBTQ rights, immigration advocacy, environmental issues, and the Me Too movement. Much of this was overdue, but I often hear expressions of surprise and disdain among members of my generation, some of whom marched in protests in their youth, about what is happening today. I was guilty of it as well. I was reminded of my mother's advice about understanding everybody's launch pad; younger generations are starting from a different place. These cross-generational conversations educated me and helped me understand the concept of collaborative silence. The failure of my generation to join in meaningful social discourse, especially in this political moment, keeps everyone's voice from being heard. Leading means listening, and you do not stop learning when you leave the classroom. It is a lifetime commitment.

GUIDING PRINCIPLE 6. *Mentors can save your life, and you will need different kinds of support at different stages of your career.* Just like my mother used to say, "Life, like the weather, has seasons, and you have to have the right clothes for each." I was fortunate to have found a series of mentors throughout my life that shaped the man and professional I became. My friends at the shoeshine stand, Uncle Zeke, Charles Hines (my sixth-grade teacher), and Earl Little (my Sunday school and choir teacher) all helped me build community. Along with my mother and father, they gave me structure and purpose. I have had dozens of other mentors, both men and women, who guided my work through college, in church, at the power plant, and at Detroit Diesel-Allison, Rolls-Royce, and Lockheed, and in my retirement. All of these people—young and old—coached me, helped me find potential growth opportunities, and urged me to fill in skill gaps. They also helped me build my tribe—a network that supported me not in the short term but for a lifetime. I am still in touch with many of them, including Carol Strange, Billy Wright, and Earl Little. Mentors invest in you and not only propel you forward professionally but also personally.

In 2008, while I was at Lockheed, I became a mentor for Shaday Woolcock, a business student at Georgia Tech who played basketball for the Yellow Jackets from 2007 to 2009 until she was injured. We met through a mutual friend at a football game and stayed connected throughout her tenure at Tech. She was a polished, thoughtful, and energetic young woman who had a promising future. Evelyn and I remained in close touch. One day right before her graduation she called me Pops. In that moment, I realized that Shaday had become family. At her graduation, she saluted her mother and then turned to salute Evelyn and me. In July 2014, she married Jahi Word-Daniels, a former Georgia Tech football player, and asked me to walk her down the aisle. I started as a mentor, evolved into a friend, and eventually became family. The men and women who mentored me did the exact same thing, and I was delighted to pay it forward with this exceptional young woman, who went on to complete her MBA at Kennesaw State University and is working on her doctorate while working for the Southern Company. Shaday, in turn, has helped me see the world through her eyes, a valuable exercise that has had a profound impact on my retirement.

GUIDING PRINCIPLE 7. *Providing someone with an opportunity is a priceless gift.* In November 1973, Chuck Alsacker, the superintendent of the shop floor at Detroit Diesel-Allison, appointed me as the first African American supervisor in his area. He was opposed to "minority hires" and made his position widely known. I knew this and tried to stay off his radar, so imagine my surprise when he presented me with this opportunity to be a supervisor. I received a substantial raise and was given new responsibility. His faith established an upward trajectory for me in the company and helped me see what was possible. I cannot repay him, but I did learn that even an intolerant person can subscribe to Dr. Martin Luther King Jr.'s adage to judge a man by the content of his character and not the color of his skin. When I became a supervisor, I tried to offer similar opportunities to my colleagues, knowing that it can make all the difference. In my personal life, I had a chance to do the same thing.

After our twin boys were born, Evelyn and I settled into a routine and life in Indianapolis, but the next summer our family made a big decision. In August 1973, Evelyn returned to Florida A&M to finish her student teaching so she could complete her undergraduate degree in education. I could have refused to let her go—telling her that I needed her help and wanted the boys to be close. This was still an era when most women who could afford to stay home with their children did so. But that seemed so selfish and wrong. Both of our parents were supportive, and Evelyn was determined to make the most of the opportunity. Several years before, my mother had urged me to ensure that Evelyn had a life and livelihood independent of me. That advice was a gift and led the way to ensuring that we were equal partners in our marriage. Evelyn became the greatest asset in my life, and it was partly because of her independence. So many of my colleagues had spouses who either faded into the background or were so dominant that they overshadowed everyone. Evelyn did neither; she was a gracious hostess and was always warm and welcoming. So much of my career was public, and it was essential to have a true partner in navigating what could sometimes be complicated social situations for both of us.

GUIDING PRINCIPLE 8. *Gifts come from unexpected places.* A few days before I graduated from college, I participated in a senior trip to DeLand, Florida. While I was gone, someone robbed our house off campus and stole the clothes I needed for my new job. My parents and I worked extra jobs all summer to scrape together enough to replace what had been lost. On the drive to the airport, my mother gave me an envelope stuffed with crumpled bills and some loose change. I did not want to take it because she had already sacrificed so much, but she insisted and said: "I'm betting my last twenty dollars on a sure thing." Her confidence was a gift, and that twenty dollars was more precious to me than almost anything else she could have given me at that moment. A similarly valuable gift would come years later from an equally remarkable woman. I was attending a Martin Luther King Jr. celebration in Atlanta in 2005 hosted by Coretta Scott King, a year before she died. Every year, Lockheed joined other corporations and organizations in sponsoring an annual citywide celebration of Atlanta's favorite son, and at the VIP reception, she and I were chatting about the events of the day for few moments. Before she left to attend to her other guests, she quietly said: "Lee, it's better to leave one year early than one year too late." We were not talking about retirement, but her comment resonated. She was the first person to encourage me to think about my exit plan, and I am still grateful for her insight.

I remember a simple but memorable gift that my boys gave me one afternoon. We were in Florida visiting my mother, and she was trying to install a set of curtains. They came with a rod system that was needlessly complex. My twin boys swung into action, and Roderick started to assemble the frame with Broderick's assistance. They were nearly finished when Roderick called me over to help with one last step that seemed to be causing them some trouble. The three of us worked on it and finally installed the curtains. Later, my mother pulled me aside and said, "Lee Ernest, you know those boys knew how to do that. They just wanted to include you." I did, and it made me feel important and needed. Our family exchanged two gifts that day—my boys helped their grandmother, and they showed me their love and respect.

I also recall one small gift that I was able to give. I pulled into a QuikTrip gas station one afternoon behind a woman who looked particularly frazzled. She had three small children in her car and was standing by the passenger door just staring at the gas pump. I went in to pay for my gas and gave him eighty dollars and told him to fill up her tank and give her the rest. Several weeks later, when I went to fill up again, the same attendant was on duty and he told me, "That lady that you helped a few weeks ago confessed to me that she was alone and only had three dollars left in her purse to pay for the gas. You really helped her, and she told me to tell you, 'God bless and Godspeed.'" Small things matter, so appreciate the gifts you have been given, and give when you can.

GUIDING PRINCIPLE 9. *Know what you do not know.* Be conscious of your incompetence, your power, and your influence. In 2000, I left Indianapolis to move to Georgia and take the helm at Lockheed Martin Aeronautical Systems Company's Marietta plant, and I knew it would be a challenge. Marietta's problems were real. The company faced discrimination lawsuits, but racism was not the only problem. I was the fifth plant chief in six years, and I arrived just as the company was laying off 2,800 workers, which reduced the workforce to 7,000. This was a stressful and uncertain time, complicated by the fact that orders for the c130j cargo plane were dwindling, and the future of the f-22 fighter program was in doubt. In this environment, I felt I had to see the problems from the employees' point of view and communicate clearly that things were going to change. I decided to schedule a series of breakfasts for hourly and salaried employees. At each breakfast, I introduced myself and then spent the rest of the time listening. I closed the breakfasts by thanking them for their candor and talked about what I was going to do in response to their concerns. I had to find out what I did not know, and these events became a direct way to receive much-needed feedback from the people who were impacted most. In total, I participated in dozens of these breakfasts, and it was the most valuable thing I ever did at the plant. It gave the workers confidence that they had been heard, and it helped me build a reputation for being someone who listened.

Most leaders do not give much thought to the relationship between power and influence. They are two different things and can affect your effectiveness and longevity in a position. The book *Organizational Behavior*, published by the University of Minnesota, includes a chapter called, "The Power to Influence." In it, the authors argue that there are six potential sources of power: legitimate (from one's organizational role or position), reward (ability to give something of value, like a raise), coercive (ability to take something away), expert (derived from knowledge or skill), information (access to specific information), and referent power (personal characteristics that attract others). While power forces someone to complete a task, influence helps them understand why that task is necessary. Influence is the bedrock of real leadership. Most leaders wonder why they are ineffective, and I would argue it's because they rely heavily on coercive power, especially when they are not experts in their field. They order their employees around and threaten them when they do not comply. Coercive power is often used to hide incompetence. But if you are conscious of your incompetence, you can draw on other more collaborative sources of power and thus extend your influence.

GUIDING PRINCIPLE 10. *Shame never breeds loyalty.* My mother knew that better than anybody. She never yelled at me or tried to embarrass me but instead asked probing questions to get me on the right path. I will never forget her asking me in the kitchen one day as I was preparing to move to Indianapolis, "How will they know you?" She wanted me to think about my brand and encouraged me to say and do the things that demonstrated that I was responsible, respectable, diligent, and worth somebody's investment. Her emotional intelligence and soft power helped me make my own way, always guided by her wisdom.

I spent my entire career working in manufacturing with active unions. These are complex work environments that are often fraught with conflict. In my early years at Detroit Diesel-Allison, Tom Ford served as union committeeman, and his issues took up an inordinate amount of my time. One afternoon on my drive home, I stopped for gas and saw him at the adjoining pump. We talked for a while, and I learned what was making his job so difficult. I am not sure if we could have had such an honest conversation at the plant. We needed a neutral environment. I discovered that the management at the plant insisted that he work for them for the first hour of the day, and Tom often had nothing to do. It was a way for management to wield power over the union. So we devised a plan that helped him accommodate leadership without losing respect among his hourly colleagues. Tom never would have been elected union committeeman if he was perceived as someone who kowtowed to management. Management would lose credibility if they gave in too easily to the union. Our plan, hatched at the gas station, helped both parties save face. My treatment of Tom also signaled to the union and to my fellow managers that there was another way to get the job done. Conflict was not inevitable; we could work together; and nobody was shamed or humiliated.

GUIDING PRINCIPLE 11. *Your assets go home at night.* The final guiding principle is in so many ways the most important. Work environments are composed of people, and most of them want to do meaningful work for good companies, but they also go home at night. I often heard in my career that the job did not matter as much as the environment in which people worked. Supervisors and management have a big responsibility to help create as positive and productive an environment as possible, and I found that utilizing the first ten principles listed above helped do just that. But it is equally important to think about what happens to your colleagues when they leave your office or plant. Do they walk out the door proud of the work they did that day? Are they inspired by their colleagues? Do they boast to their friends and family about how much they like their job? Do they show up early, stay late, and use their vacation and sick time when needed? Do they volunteer to take on new projects or difficult assignments? Do they seize opportunities for additional education or training? Do they actively seek mentors or serve as mentors? Do they help their communities? Do they make suggestions about how to improve company operations? Do they apply for or seek promotions? Do they retire with grace and dignity? If so, you have done more than help them make a living. You helped them make a life. And I hope that in my career that I did just that.

ACKNOWLEDGMENTS

FROM LEE

I have torn up dozens of pieces of paper trying to write these acknowledgments. It is never difficult to thank people who helped me; my fear is that I might forget somebody.

I have been working on this book project for years but never quite got to the finish line. My brother recently passed away, and the reminder of my own mortality helped jump-start the process in the fall of 2018. I wanted to write this book, not because I had an extraordinary story, but because I thought I had learned a few things that might help readers as they embark or reflect on their own journeys. The challenge was finding the right partner—and that came in the form of a tip from Dr. Kathy Schwaig, provost at Kennesaw State University.

Kat and I came to know each other when she was dean at the Coles College of Business, and we have developed a deep and abiding friendship that I treasure. I called her after my brother passed away and told her I was ready to start the project in earnest. That is when she told me to call Dr. Catherine Lewis. Catherine is a historian and the assistant vice president for museums, archives, and rare books at Kennesaw State. She has written more than a dozen books and recently completed one with Michael Coles entitled *Time to Get Tough: How Cookies, Coffee, and a Crash Led to Success in Business and Life.*

In our first meeting, we talked about a wide range of topics, and it became instantly clear that Catherine both knew my story and had the ability to put it into broad historical context. She also helped me think about the book in an unconventional way. The first draft chapters, before I started working with Catherine, were written for a business school audience and were fairly technical. We were making progress, but it just never felt right. It was the story of Lee E. Rhyant, corporate executive. I think that is why it stalled. Catherine helped me understand that the story needed balance—the story of Lee Ernest Rhyant, son, friend, brother, parent, and husband could be combined with the story of Lee E. Rhyant to provide a more complete picture of my life and guiding principles. I knew in the first five minutes with Catherine that I had found the perfect partner, and I was right. I am so grateful that she agreed to join me on this journey. We started as colleagues and ended up as family.

I believe that the person I have become is the culmination of those who helped mold and shape me. I have been fortunate to have a long list of family, friends, and mentors: Harding and Evelyn Rhyant, Buster and Louise Ingram, Billy Wright, Bob Brown, Charles Hines, Earl Little, Jerry Cooper, Uncle Zeke, Maxwell King, Carole Strange, Clayton Grier, Emmett Barnes, Ernest Ghent, Broderick McKinney, George Miller, Coryendon "Buzz" Nurse, Professor Thomas Demps, Otis Watson, Charles Cherry, A. J. Jackson, Hudner Hobbs, Bob Beasecker, Ted Hadley, Joe White, Eddie Off, Robert "Bob" Hicks, Chris and Ralph Tolan, Tom Ford, Cleo Miller, Tim Higgins, Ernest Vaughn, Crawford Loritts, Robert McCallum, Tim Ross, Dan Duncan, Pat Laughlin, Willie Bonner, Dennis Sumpter, Kenny Doss, Wilson Burns, Jim Lunsford, F. Blake Wallace, John Ferry, Hamilton Holmes Jr., Shan Cooper, Jack Lambert, Tim McDonald, Harris Travis, Winston Strickland, Ambassador Andrew Young, John Lewis, Deanne Bonner, Joseph Lowery, Shirley Franklin, Roy Barnes, Winston Strickland, Otis Brumby, Bob Moultrie, Saxby Chambliss, Phil Gingrey, Coretta Scott King, Robert "Bob" Stevens, Ralph and Janet Heath, Bill Shoemaker, Shaday Word-Daniels, Dale Gordon, Cheyenne Cheetam, Alyce Sarno, Sam and Lisa Olens, Karla Washington, Sandy and Harry Gurnell, Jackie and Leroy Greenwood, Carl and Jackie Parks, the Reverend Orville Sutton, Uncle John Lee, Chris Kubasik, Margie Houston, Louise Houston, Rebecca Ingram, Charles and Eva McIntyre, Robin Brewington, Harry Miller, Sam Woolford, Cheryl and Gary Jackson,

Donovan Wells, the boys and men at the shoeshine stand in Fort Pierce, Godfrey Saunders, Tony Stone, Archie Stanley, Joe Booth, Wilma Walker, Elaine Jacks, Janet Long, Norma Davenport, Dennis and Carmelita Marrow, Willie B. and Beverly Matthews, Alyce and Bill Sarno, Margie Houston, Louise Houston, Doris Wright, Janine Ingram Bryant, Eddie Evens, Calvin Henderson, William Knowles, John Logan, William "Willie" Webb, Terry Powell, Mac and Laurel Stevenson, Gary and Lois Bailey, Kasim Reed, Benny and Viola Rhyant, Virginia and Ron Goodwin, Deleah and Jenelle Goodwin, Herb and Shelia Tucker, Charles and Fabiola Crain, Sonny and Phyllis Wyatt, Charles and Eva McIntyre, Jim and Celia Thomas, Edward Ingram, Clarence Ingram, Melvin Ingram, Jonathan Ingram, Rick and Janet Ramsey, Linton and Bridget Davis, Mike and Carolyn Malone, Cheryl Ash-Simpson, Tom Moore, JuLee Childre, Berena Paschal, Nelson and Sonya McCray, George and Dorothy Johnson, Latasha Brinson, Cathryn Rhyant, Deidre Gainey, Debbie Wright Johnson, Darlena Wright, Dorie Tuggle, Nancy Rhyant, Abby Smith Lilly, Thomas and Odessa Rhyant, Joan Cooper, Renee and Vivian Cooper, Mary and Randy Toombs, Fannie Mae Gardner, Terry and Rebecca Powell, Linda Gooden, Lorraine Martin, Greg Ulmer, James and Cecelia Thomas, Jeff Babione, Rachael White Ranor, Michael and Shirley Fluckus, Don and Eva Johnson, Brenda Johnson, Rozalyne Penix Wright, John Culmer, Dorothy Jean Rhyant, Michelle D. Gillis, Gerome Rhyant, Thomas Rhyant, James Rhyant, Tyronne Rhyant, Leroy and Karen Governor, Kia and Gregg Palmer, Richard and Sharon Rhyant, Prinest Paschal, Allison Cobb, Sarah Smith, Debbie and Ross Reynolds, Mike O'Brian, Gregory Smith, Francine Smith, Angela Garder, Alphonso Gardner, Candace Laye, Sammie and Tereasa Gaines, Carolyn Houston, Lucy Sharpe, Carolyn Banks, Mildred Jones Neal, Vance Coffman, Barbara and Audrey Reynolds, Charles and Eva McIntyre, Pamela Whitten, Kathy "Kat" Schwaig, Robin Cheramie, Brianna Gainey, Kessell Stelling, Milton Oberton, Dale Gordon, Thomas Emmerson, Gabrielle "Gabby" Rhyant, Zachariah Rhyant, Jeremiah Rhyant, Broderick and Andrea Rhyant, and Roderick and Anjulia Rhyant.

Numerous institutions shaped me in profound ways, including

the faculty and students at Lincoln Park Academy, especially the class of 1968, Mt. Moriah Primitive Baptist Church, Crooked Creek Baptist Church, the Marietta Operations Committee at Lockheed Marietta, Westside Christian Schools, Heritage Christian Schools, Butler University, Kelly School of Business at Indiana University, Bethune-Cookman University and their concert chorale, the University of Dayton, the City of Fort Pierce, Lockheed Martin, Rolls-Royce Aerospace, Allison Engine Company, Omega Psi Phi, Indian River College, Florida A&M University, the University of Georgia, and the Coles College of Business at Kennesaw State University. There are so many others whose names have been lost to history who also supported me in innumerable ways.

I want to extend a special thanks to Senator Johnny Isakson for writing the foreword. His distinguished career in real estate and later in the House of Representatives and the U.S. Senate has made the state of Georgia a great place to live. We met when I became executive vice president and general manager for the Marietta facility of Lockheed Martin Aeronautics Company. Our decades-long friendship is something I treasure, and I am so grateful that he agreed to be part of this project. I also owe a special thanks to Kat Schwaig, who wrote the prologue. Kat has been an exceptional leader in her field and has helped Kennesaw State University grow and thrive. She is a dear friend and colleague, and I am eternally grateful for her contribution.

Writing a memoir is a very personal exercise, and it has been a very emotional process. I remember one afternoon, about four months into the process, I found myself walking through a local park in Roswell to reflect on the whole process. It forces you to reflect on your successes, and also your failures, lost opportunities, and regrets. I had plenty of both, but I also felt an overwhelming sense of gratitude—for everything that I had learned and for the people who enriched my life. Nobody has been more important than my family. Evelyn, my beloved wife and most ardent supporter, helped make everything possible. She is smart, compassionate, and tough as nails. Her confidence and strong faith made sure that our family was going to succeed. My twin sons, Broderick and Roderick, have been a great source of love and pride. I could not have asked for better children and could not be prouder of the men, fathers, and physicians that they have become. I learned as much from them as they did from me. They have helped me bring this book to fruition, and I will forever be grateful for their love and support. I dedicate this book to them.

FROM CATHERINE

This book grew out of an email exchange with Dr. Kathy Schwaig, provost at Kennesaw State University. I had recently finished a book, *Time to Get Tough: How Cookies, Coffee, and a Crash Led to Success in Business and in Life* with Michael Coles, the namesake of the Coles College of Business, where Kat served as the former dean. It was a great project, and we were in the midst of a multiyear book tour to help promote it. On November 11, 2018, Kat sent me the following message: "Hi Catherine, Lee Rhyant wants to write a book. Former head of Lockheed Marietta. Sharecropper's son. Played basketball one day with MLK when he was a boy. Amazing story. Leadership book." I knew the broad outlines of Lee's story, so I reached out, and we agreed to meet on November 28 on campus before he was scheduled to attend an Athletic Board meeting. At 11:00 a.m., we met in a classroom in the Bagwell College of Education. In the first five minutes, I knew this would be a great project. Lee has a terrific story and a particularly engaging way of telling it. He is also one of the nicest people I have ever met; I instantly felt like I was talking to a favorite cousin or uncle. We started on the project immediately, and *Soaring* is the result of all of our hard work.

We had a number of people help us along the way. Amy Henley, formerly the executive director of MBA Programs at KSU and now the dean of the University of North Dakota's College of Business and Public Administration, had worked with Lee for several years on a book project, and she graciously shared her insights. Dennis Marrow, a close friend and colleague of Lee's who also worked on the first book project, became an invaluable resource. He offered numerous insightful stories and suggestions, and he served as a terrific editor for the manuscript in its early iterations. Librarians, archivists, and scholars around the country helped with various components of the book, and special recognition belongs to Matt Holdzkom, assistant reference librarian at the Indiana Historical Society. He helped tease out some of the complicated history of Allison Engine Company.

Coming to know Lee also means that you get to know his family, his wife, Evelyn, and his two sons, Broderick and Roderick. They became essential partners for this book—making suggestions, reading drafts, and offering the kind of support you need to bring a big story like this to fruition. My only regret is that writing a book during the COVID-19 pandemic meant that we had to do most of our work virtually, and I missed our lunches in the conference room and hallway chats. But we quickly pivoted to socially distanced visits in the driveway to keep connected and exchange oatmeal raisin cookies.

The team at the University of Georgia helped shepherd the book into publication. It is always a pleasure to work with Lisa Bayer and her team, and this is my third book with them. They are wonderful partners who do so much to help promote scholarship and the history of the state. We were delighted to work with the press and so very happy with the final result.

My final thanks go to friends and family who read so many drafts and made useful suggestions. My husband, John Companiotte, is an excellent editor and distinguished author in his own right. My colleagues at Kennesaw State University, notably Tyler Crafton-Karnes, Stefanie Green, and Kate Marchman, became sounding boards. But my real debt goes to my father, Dr. James Richard Lewis, who has been a mentor and collaborator on numerous book projects. He taught me more than I can ever repay and had been an invaluable editor for every book I have written, including this one. I am a historian because of him and am eternally grateful for his many contributions. He passed away in November 2020, and I love and miss him dearly. I dedicate this book to him.

SELECTED BIBLIOGRAPHY

Allen, Reniqua. "The Missing Black Millennial." *New Republic*, February 20, 2019.

Allison. *Allison: Yesterday, Today, and Tomorrow*. Speedway, Ind.: Allison Division of General Motors, 1983.

Alsobrook, David E. *Southside: Eufaula's Cotton Mill Village and Its People, 1890–1945*. Macon, Ga.: Mercer University Press, 2017.

Augustine, Norman R. "Reshaping an Industry: Lockheed Martin's Survival Story." *Harvard Business Review*, May–June 1997.

Blackmon, Douglas. *Slavery by Another Name: The Re-enslavement of Black People in America from the Civil War to World War II*. New York: Anchor, 2008.

Calhoun, Ada. "Gen-X Women Are Caught in a Generational Tug of War." *Atlantic*, January 2020.

Cauley, H. M. "Retiring Won't Ground Charitable Efforts." *Atlanta Journal-Constitution*, October 24, 2010, E14.

Cavazos, Shaina. "Racial Bias and the Crumbling of a City." *Atlantic*, August 17, 2016.

Chamberlin, Jamie. "Retiring Minds Want to Know." *Monitor on Psychology* 45, no. 1 (January 2014): 61.

Coles, Michael, and Catherine Lewis. *Time to Get Tough: How Cookies, Coffee, and a Crash Led to Success in Business and Life*. Athens: University of Georgia Press, 2018.

Davis, Mark. "Wartime Wings Lifted City." *Atlanta Journal-Constitution*, May 24, 2009.

Dine, Phillip. "Black Workers File Bias Suit against Lockheed Martin." *St. Louis Post-Dispatch*, May 11, 2000, A11.

Duncan, Roger Dean. "Are You a (Former) Boss Who Just Won't Go Away?" *Forbes*, April 12, 2018.

Evanoff, Ted. "Allison Changes Gears with the Times." *Indianapolis Star*, August 5, 2002, C1.

——— . "Aviation Helped Allison Take Off." *Indianapolis Star*, August 5, 2002, C2.

Feigen, Marc A., and Ron Williams. "The CEO's Guide to Retirement." *Harvard Business Review*, September 14, 2018.

Flanigan, Eugene, and Daniel Nigro. *Field Experience with Detroit Diesel-Allison 404–405 Industrial Gas Turbine Engines*. Warrendale, Pa.: Society of Automotive Engineers, 1979.

Flatt, William P. "Agriculture in Georgia: Overview." *New Georgia Encyclopedia*, November 2, 2020.

Florida Stories. "A Dream of Education, a Vision of Hope, and the Strive for Excellence." https://floridastories.oncell.com/en/lincoln-park-academy -176586.html.

Gant, Andrew. "B-CU Grads Get Surprise Gift, Sound Advice." *Daytona Beach News-Journal*, December 9, 2012.

General Motors Corporation. *History of Allison Gas Turbine Division*. Indianapolis, Ind.: General Motors Corporation, Detroit Diesel-Allison Division, 1984.

Gillooly, Jon. "A Fond Farewell, a Hearty Hello." *Marietta Daily Journal*, March 23, 2001.

Goodwin, Doris Kearns. *Team of Rivals: The Political Genius of Abraham Lincoln*. New York: Simon and Shuster, 2006.

Grillo, Jerry. "Departures and Arrivals: A Changing of the Guard." *Georgia Trend*, March 2011.

Halbfinger, David M. "Man Kills Five Co-Workers at Plant and Himself." *New York Times*, July 9, 2003.

Hirschman, Dave. "Lockheed Told of Strike Date: Mediators Will Try to Help Craft Deal." *Atlanta Journal-Constitution*, March 5, 2002, D1.

———. "Lockheed Union Gets New Offer: Strike Hangs on Sunday Vote." *Atlanta Journal-Constitution*, March 9, 2002.

———. "Machinists Put Lockheed on Strike Alert." *Atlanta Journal-Constitution*, March 2, 2005, C1.

———. "Strikers Return to Job Quietly." *Atlanta Journal Constitution*, March 17, 2005, E3.

———. "Union Urged Not to Strike." *Atlanta Journal Constitution*, March 5, 2005, G1.

Holusha, John. "Reshaping the Arms Industry." *New York Times*, August 31, 1994, A1.

Hurston, Zora Neale. "Florida's Migrant Farm Labor." *Frontiers: A Journal of Women Studies* 12, no. 1 (1991): 199–203.

Johnson, J. Douglas. "Allison Takes Off." *Indiana Business Magazine*, March 1994, 8.

Kirkpatrick, Karen. "Flight Commander." *Georgia Trend* 30, no. 9 (May 2015).

Koenig, Bill. "Allison Engine Sees Cost Cutting in Future." *Indianapolis Star*, December 3, 1993, F1.

———. "Allison Transmission Chief Steps Down." *Indianapolis Star*, December 29, 1993, B1.

———. "GM Slims Down." *Indianapolis Star*, November 15, 1992, B1.

———. "It's an Engine for Growth." *Indianapolis Star*, July 3, 1998, C1.

———. "Justice Department Sues to Block Sale of Allison." *Indianapolis Star*, November 17, 1993, A1.

"Lockheed Martin's Lee Rhyant Recognized as NMA Executive of the Year." *PR Newswire*, September 16, 2009.

McCue, T. J. "Fifty-Seven Million U.S. Workers Are Part of the Gig Economy." *Forbes*, August 31, 2018. https://www.forbes.com/sites/tjmccue/2018/08/31/57-million-u-s-workers-are-part-of-the-gig-economy/?sh=75e3833c7118.

McGeehan, Patrick. "Dealing with Aging Executives Who Just Won't Quit," *New York Times*, February 2, 2003.

McGirt, Ellen. "Leading While Black: An Inside Look at What's Keeping Black Men Out of the Executive Suite." *Fortune*, January 22, 2016.

McKeand, Patrick. "Allison's Seventy-Fifth." *Indiana Business*, September 1, 1990, 20.

Mahler, Jonathan. "GM, Detroit, and the Fall of the Black Middle Class." *New York Times*, June 24, 2009.

Marcus, Bernie, and Arthur Blank. *Built from Scratch: How a Couple of Regular Guys Grew the Home Depot from Nothing to $30 Billion.* New York: Currency, 2001.

Martin, Carolyn A., and Bruce Tulgan. *Managing the Generation Mix: From Urgency to Opportunity.* Amherst: HRD Press, 2006.

Melvin, Don. "New Offensive in the Defense Industry." *Atlanta Journal-Constitution*, June 23, 1995.

Menon, Tanya, and Leigh Thompson. "Putting a Price on People Problems at Work." *Harvard Business Review*, August 23, 2016.

Mitchell, Dawn. "Fifty Years Ago the Justice Department Sued IPS to Force Desegregation." *Indianapolis Star*, May 31, 2018.

Moore, Leonard J. *Citizen Klansmen: The Ku Klux Klan in Indiana, 1921–1928.* Chapel Hill: University of North Carolina Press, 1991.

"Nineteen-Sixty-Eight: The Year That Shattered America." *Smithsonian*, January–February 2018.

O'Neill, Thomas P. "Frenemies: A Love Story." *New York Times*, October 5, 2012.

Organizational Behavior. Minneapolis: University of Minnesota, 2017.

Owen, C. James, and York Willbern. *Governing Metropolitan Indianapolis: The Politics of Unigov.* Berkeley: University of California Press, 1985.

Parent, Tawn. "Allison Sale: Is Transmission Division a Bargain at $500 Million?" *Indiana Business Journal*, January 20, 1992, 1.

——. "Ripe for Picking? Allison Sale Will Follow Decade of Heavy Investment." *Indiana Business Journal*, April 13, 1992, 1.

Parsons, Keith. "First Strike in Twenty-Five Years." *Associated Press*, March 11, 2002.

Pasmore, Bill, Cindy McCauley, Alice Cahill, Mike Smith, Chuck Ainswroth, and Chuck Palus. "Turning Crisis into Opportunity: Preparing Your Organization for a Transformed World." Greensboro, N.C.: Center for Creative Leadership, 2020.

Patton, Randall. *Lockheed, Atlanta, and the Struggle for Racial Integration*. Athens: University of Georgia Press, 2019.

Peltz, James F. "Trial by Fire Left Lockheed a Strong Survivor." *Los Angeles Times*, August 30, 1994.

Peralte, Paul. "Lockheed to Cut 675 More Jobs." *Atlanta Journal-Constitution*, January 4, 2001, K1.

Pickel, Mary Lou. "Home at Last: Dismantled Navy Spy Plane Back at Marietta Facility." *Atlanta Journal-Constitution*, July 5, 2001.

——. "Lockheed Workers Fear Closing." *Atlanta Journal-Constitution*, March 22, 2001, XJG1.

Politico. "Coronavirus Will Change the World Permanently. Here's How." *Politico*, March 19, 2020.

Powell, Colin. *It Worked for Me: In Life and Leadership*. New York: Harper Perennial, 2014.

Rhyant, Lee. "Opinion: Lockheed Martin Is Taking Georgia's Aerospace Industry to New Altitudes." *Marietta Daily Journal*, September 16, 2010.

Rogers, Carol. "Black and White in Indiana." *Indiana Business Review* (Summer 2005).

Rowling, J. K. *Harry Potter and the Sorcerer's Stone*. New York: Scholastic, 1998.

Schneider, Greg. "Lockheed Now Faces the Onus of Healing." *Atlanta Journal-Constitution*, May 5, 2002, Q1.

——. "Lockheed's Latest Battle." *Washington Post*, July 16, 2000, H1.

——. "Lockheed: Some Workers Agree." *Washington Post*, March 9, 2002, A7.

——. "Lockheed Strikers Called Orderly." *Atlanta Journal-Constitution*, (March 15, 2002): F3.

——. "Lockheed Union Gets New Offer." *Atlanta Journal-Constitution*, March 9, 2002, F1.

Scott, Thomas. "Lockheed Martin." *New Georgia Encyclopedia*, June 8, 2017.

Simons, John. "Where Are All the Black CEOs?" *Wall Street Journal*, May 21, 2018.

Squeo, Anne Marie. "Lockheed Plant in Georgia Sees a Turnaround." *Wall Street Journal*, July 7, 2000, A4.

Sullivan, Louis, and David Chanoff. *Breaking Ground: My Life in Medicine.* Athens: University of Georgia Press, 2016.

Taylor, Robert A. "In the Interests of Justice: The Burial of Pondexteur Eugene Williams." *Florida Historical Quarterly* 82, no. 3 (Winter 2004): 273–88.

Tharpe, Jim. "Raptor Boss Has Roots in Georgia Soil." *Atlanta Journal-Constitution*, May 9, 2009, D1.

Thornbrough, Emma Lou. "The Indianapolis Story: School Segregation and Desegregation in a Northern City." Unpublished manuscript, Indiana Historical Society, 1993.

Thurston, Scott. "Black Executive to Run Lockheed Marietta Plant." *Atlanta Journal-Constitution*, May 13, 2000, E1.

———. "Lockheed Martin Plant Greets Leader." *Atlanta Journal-Constitution*, July 12, 2000, 3B.

Visser, Steve. "Eleven at Lockheed Tile Two Racial Bias Suits." *Atlanta Journal-Constitution*, May 11, 2000, E1.

Walsh, Mary Williams. "U.S. Joins in Bias Suits against Lockheed Martin." *New York Times*, December 6, 2000, C1.

Webb, Jon. "Opinion: Indiana Still Has a Racism Problem." *Evansville Courier and Press*, November 7, 2017.

"West-Central Indiana's Largest Employer." *Indiana Business*, October 1988, 68.

ABOUT THE AUTHORS

LEE RHYANT was raised in the Jim Crow South and overcame numerous obstacles to reach the executive ranks at General Motors, Rolls-Royce Aeronautics, and Lockheed Martin. From 2000 to 2011, he served as executive vice president and general manager for Lockheed Martin in Marietta. Since leaving the aerospace industry, Lee has been highly sought after as an executive coach and confidant to Fortune 500 executives across the industrial spectrum. His leadership has earned him numerous business, community, and congressional accolades. Lee is a member of the advisory board at Kennesaw State University, Georgia's second largest and fastest-growing university, and is an executive in residence at the Coles College of Business at Kennesaw State University. He is the president and CEO of LER Solutions, LLC, an executive coaching firm in Atlanta.

DR. CATHERINE M. LEWIS is assistant vice president of museums, archives, and rare books; director of the Museum of History and Holocaust Education; and professor of history at Kennesaw State University. She is the author, coeditor, or coauthor of fifteen books, including *Don't Ask What I Shot: How Eisenhower's Love of Golf Helped Shape 1950s America* (McGraw Hill, 2007) and *Time to Get Tough: How Cookies, Coffee, and a Crash Led to Success in Business and Life* (University of Georgia Press, 2018) with Michael J. Coles. Dr. Lewis has curated more than forty exhibits for organizations around the nation including Delta Air Lines, United Way, and Augusta National Golf Club. She regularly presents at national and international conferences and serves on numerous boards, including the Women's Leadership Committee at Kennesaw State University, the Yates Scholarship Board for the Georgia State Golf Association, and the Museum Committee for the United States Golf Association. In 2018, she was named chair of the Robert T. Jones Jr. Program, a partnership between Emory University and the University of St. Andrews.